APR. 03

Partial Results from Prototype Testing Efforts for Disk Imaging Tools: SafeBack 2.0

NCJ 199000

NIJ

Sarah V. Hart
Director

This report was prepared for the National Institute of Justice, U.S. Department of Justice, by the Office of Law Enforcement Standards of the National Institute of Standards and Technology under Interagency Agreement 94–IJ–R–004.

The National Institute of Justice is a component of the Office of Justice Programs, which also includes the Bureau of Justice Assistance, the Bureau of Justice Statistics, the Office of Juvenile Justice and Delinquency Prevention, and the Office for Victims of Crime.

Introduction

The Computer Forensics Tool Testing (CFTT) project is the joint effort of the National Institute of Justice, the National Institute of Standards and Technology (NIST), the U.S. Department of Defense, the Technical Support Working Group, and other related agencies. The objective of the CFTT project is to provide measurable assurance to practitioners, researchers, and other applicable users that the tools used in computer forensics investigations provide accurate results. Accomplishing this requires the development of specifications and test methods for computer forensics tools and subsequent testing of specific tools against those specifications.

The test results provide the information necessary for developers to improve tools, users to make informed choices, and the legal community and others to understand the tools' capabilities. The use of well-recognized methodologies for conformance and quality testing serves as the foundation of our approach for testing computer forensics tools. Plus, in an effort to further develop the specifications and test methods, we encourage the entire forensics community to visit the CFTT Web site (*http://www.cftt.nist.gov*), where drafts are accessible for both commentary and review.

This document reports partial results obtained during prototype testing efforts. Those efforts were part of the development of the test methodology and the support software for testing disk imaging software. The product used for test development was SafeBack version 2.0. The disk imaging specification and the test cases were early versions of the specifications now in use and available on the Web site. In addition, the support software and the testing procedures were prototype versions. The test results are presented here, however, to disseminate information about a few test cases that may still be of interest for those using older versions of the SafeBack software. For those using a newer version, see the test report on SafeBack version 2.18, available early in 2003.

Partial Results from Prototype Testing Efforts

for Disk Imaging Tools

Tool Tested: SafeBack
Version: 2.0 (January 31, 2000)
Operating System: PC DOS 6.30
Supplier: New Technologies, Inc. (SafeBack formerly owned by Sydex, Incorporated)
Address: 2075 NE Division Street
                    Gresham, OR 97030
Phone: 503–661–6912   Web: *http://www.forensics-intl.com*

1. Partial Results Summary by Requirements

The tool shall not alter the original disk.
For all of the test cases that were run, an SHA-1 hash was created on the source, the test case was run, and an SHA-1 hash was created on the source after the run. In all cases the hash codes matched (i.e., the source was not altered).

The tool shall make a bit-stream duplicate or an image of an original disk or partition.
For most cases tested, SafeBack produced a complete and accurate bit-stream duplicate or an image on disks or partitions of all disk sectors copied. However, if a legacy BIOS interface that underreports the disk size was used, not all of the sectors on the disk were copied. Also, if a direct disk copy was used on an SCSI disk using an ASPI driver, only a small portion of the sectors was copied.

The tool shall log I/O errors.
In whole-disk test cases involving a read error, write error, or corrupt image error, SafeBack flagged the error and generated an error message in the SafeBack log. Test cases involving partitions were not tested sufficiently to report here.

The tool's documentation shall be correct.
Documentation available for testing this version of SafeBack was somewhat inconclusive or incomplete, so identification of expected behavior was not always possible.

2. Anomalies

Of the test cases that were applied to SafeBack 2.0, these were the detected anomalies:

1. If an entire physical disk is duplicated on a larger physical disk, SafeBack allows the specification of either filling the remainder of the destination with zeros or leaving the destination as is. In two test cases [DI-11 and DI-22], SafeBack performed some zero filling when the requested option was to leave the remainder of the disk as is.

2. If SafeBack is used to copy a physical disk to another physical disk of a different geometry, SafeBack optionally can reposition partitions to disk cylinder boundaries. The partition repositioning changes the contents of the first sector of each partition as documented but also repositions the last sector of the source partition to the last position of the destination partition. This anomaly was noted in four test cases [DI-03, DI-07, DI-14, and DI-18].

3. If a disk is being accessed by the BIOS, and the physical source disk contains more than 1,024 cylinders, and the BIOS presents an adjusted (logical) disk geometry with fewer than 1,024 cylinders by increasing the heads per cylinder value, then the tool accesses one more logical cylinder beyond the last disk cylinder indicated by the BIOS. For example, the Quantum Sirocco model 1700 has the following direct physical and BIOS access parameters:

Access	Cylinders	Heads	Sectors per Head	Sectors per Cylinder	Total Sectors
Direct	3,309	16	63	1,008	3,335,472
BIOS	826	64	63	4,032	3,330,432

Note that 5,040 more sectors can be accessed by direct access than by BIOS access. Consider test case DI-04: The expected value for the **Data Filled** column is 0; however, the actual value is 4,032. SafeBack copied one extra BIOS cylinder (4,032 sectors) but missed the last physical cylinder of 1,008 sectors.

Consider test case DI-74: SafeBack was executed using BIOS access, but all the physical disk sectors were compared. The 1,008 sectors that differ are the last physical cylinder, missed by SafeBack. This anomaly was noted in 9 test cases [DI-03, DI-04, DI-07, DI-11, DI-14, DI-15, DI-18, DI-22, and DI-74]. Using direct access eliminates this BIOS problem, as in test case DI-75 where the entire physical disk was copied and no sectors were missed.

4. A direct SCSI disk copy, using the ASPI driver for the SCSI adapter, copied only 2,097,270 sectors from a source disk with 17,921,835 sectors to an equal-size disk, leaving 15,824,565 sectors of the destination disk unchanged. SafeBack gave no indication of any problems and indicated a successful copy [DI-79].

Other observed behavior
A SafeBack image file contains all the data read from the imaged source plus cyclical redundancy checksums (CRC) for verifying the integrity of the captured data. If SafeBack is restoring a source

to a destination from an image file, an automatic verification of the CRC is performed. When SafeBack is trying to restore to a destination disk that is smaller than the source, as in test cases DI-13, DI-60, and DI-61, the verification message is missing from the tool log file.

3. Testing Environment

The primary testing environment consists of six different platforms: beta-1, beta-2, beta-3, beta-4, beta-5, and beta-6.

Beta-1, beta-2, beta-3, and beta-4
Beta-1, beta-2, beta-3, and beta-4 are identical Nexar 166MHz computers with 256MB RAM; two hard disk drive bays, both of which take hard drives mounted in removable carriages; a CD–ROM drive; a 1.44MB floppy drive; and a 17-inch color monitor. The usual operating system environment is DOS 6.30, booted from the floppy drive. The BIOS is Award v4.51PG.

Beta-5
Beta-5 is a Dell Computer Corporation system with 256MB RAM, one hard disk drive bay, one installed 15.37 GB hard disk, a CD–ROM drive, a 1.44MB floppy drive, a 250MB ZIP drive, and a 17-inch color monitor. The usual operating system environment is DOS 6.30, booted from the floppy drive. The BIOS is PhoenixBios 4.0 Release 6.0.

Beta-6
Beta-6 is a Nexar 166MHz computer with 256MB RAM, two SCSI hard disks (C0 and C1), a CD–ROM drive, a 1.44MB floppy drive, and a 17-inch color monitor. The SCSI adapter is the Adaptec AHA-2940UW Pro with SCSI BIOS V2.11.0. The usual operating system environment is DOS 6.30, booted from the floppy drive. The BIOS is Award v4.51PG.

Disks
The following disks were used on the machines listed above for the testing procedures. For all but two of these disks, the actual physical disk contains more than 1,024 cylinders. Although the maximum number of heads physically possible is 16, the BIOS presents an adjusted logical disk geometry with fewer than 1,024 cylinders by increasing the heads per cylinder value.

Label	Model	Use	Cyl	Hd	Sec	Total Sectors	MB
D1	Quantum Sirocco 1700A	DOS source	826	64	63	3,330,432	1,705
D2	Quantum Sirocco 1700A	Destination	826	64	63	3,330,432	1,705
D3	Fujitsu MPE3064AT	Dest or image media	787	255	63	12,643,155	6,473
D4	Quantum Sirocco 1700A	Linux source	826	64	63	3,330,432	1,705
D5	Seagate	Destination	619	64	63	2,495,808	1,277
D7	Quantum Sirocco 1700A	Destination	826	64	63	3,330,432	1,705
D9	Quantum Sirocco 1700A	SmWinNT src	826	64	63	3,330,432	1,705
D11	Fujitsu MPE3064AT	Dest or image media	787	255	63	12,643,155	6,473
F1	Quantum Sirocco 1700A	Win 95 src	826	64	63	3,330,432	1,705
F2	Quantum Sirocco 1700A	Win 98 src	826	64	63	3,330,432	1,705
B0	Fujitsu MPF3153AT	Destination	16,383	16	63	30,023,280	1,537
B1	Fujitsu MPF3153AT	W2000 lrg NTFS src	16,383	16	63	30,023,280	1,537
C0	Seagate ST39204	No OS, source	SCSI			17,921,835	9,176
C1	Seagate ST39204	Destination	SCSI			17,921,835	9,176

4. Analysis of Test Results

This section presents a tabular summary of the test results. A description of the tabular layout is presented first, followed by a discussion of the expected results and tabular summary.

Summary Table Layout
The summary table contains one row of information for each test case. The columns are as follows:

Case	The test case identifier.	
Parameters	The parameters specified for this test case.	
	P--------	Operation on a physical device (i.e., an entire disk).
	L--------	Operation on a logical device (i.e., a partition).
	-C-------	Copy directly from source to destination.
	-I-------	Create an image file from the source then restore to the destination.
	-V-------	Verify an image file.
	--B------	Use BIOS access.
	--D------	Use direct access.
	--S------	Use BIOS access to SCSI disk.
	--A------	Use the SCSI adapter driver for direct access to an SCSI disk.
	---D-----	DOS source disk with FAT12 and small FAT16.
	---5-----	Windows 95 source disk with big FAT16.
	---8-----	Windows 98 source disk with FAT32.
	---N-----	Windows NT source disk with NTFS.
	---0-----	Windows 2000 with NTFS and FAT32 on 15GB disk.
	---L-----	Linux source disk.
	---------	No OS loaded, no partition table.
	----=----	Source and destination are the same size.
	----<----	Source is smaller than destination.
	---->----	Source is larger than destination.
	-----F---	Zero-fill excess space on the destination.
	------A--	Adjust partitions to cylinder boundaries.
	-------L-	Use a communications link between two machines.
	--------SR	Force a read error on the source.
	--------IW	Force a write error to the image file.
	--------IR	Force a read error from the image file.
	--------IC	Use a corrupted image file.
	--------DW	Force a write error to the destination.

Messages	Code	Messages in the tool log file.
	C	Checksum does not match expected value.
	E	I/O error occurred.
	S	Source is larger than destination.
	V	Checksum matches (verifies) the expected value.
Src Total	Total number of sectors on the source disk or partition.	
Compared	Total number of sectors compared.	
Match	Number of corresponding sectors that have the same content.	
Differ	Number corresponding sectors that have at least one bit different.	
Lost	Number of source sectors without a corresponding destination sector.	
Dst Total	Total number of sectors on the destination disk or partition.	
Zero Fill	Total number of zero-filled excess sectors.	
Data Filled	Total number of excess sectors containing a fill pattern from the DISKWIPE program.	
Not Filled	Total number of remaining excess sectors.	
Notes	The note indicates one of the following: 1. Zero-fill anomaly. 2. A checksum verifies message is missing from the log file. 3. Cylinder adjustment anomaly. 4. BIOS anomaly. 5. SCSI anomaly. e/r Expected result obtained.	

Expected Results

The expected results referenced in the summary table can be grouped into eight categories:

1. If a source is copied to a destination, either directly or indirectly, and there are no I/O errors, then corresponding sectors compare equal. If there are no I/O errors, then the expected result is for the **Differ** column to have a value of 0. This applies to test cases DI-01, DI-02, DI-03, DI-04, DI-05, DI-10, DI-25, DI-32, DI-33, DI-39, DI-40, DI-75, and DI-76. This also applies to the following test assertions: 1–3, 6–10, 12–16, 18–19, and 33–35.

   If a read or write I/O error is a test parameter, then a sector address is selected, and a Terminate and Stay Resident (TSR) program monitors all disk requests. An attempt to perform the I/O operation that includes the selected sector returns a failure code to the tool. If the tool is able to recover from the I/O failure, then a block of sectors on the destination that would have contained the selected sector if there had been no I/O error should fail to compare equal. The number of sectors in the block varies depending on the type of error, type of SafeBack operation, and location of the I/O error. For example, a read error of a single source sector may only affect one sector, but a read error of an image file sector that contains a checksum may cause an entire block of 119 sectors to be omitted from the destination. This applies to test cases DI-06, DI-07, DI-08, DI-09, DI-22, and DI-24.

   If the source is larger than the destination, the size difference is reflected in the **Lost** column. This applies to test cases DI-2, DI-13, DI-39, DI-40, DI-60, DI-61, and DI-76.

There is a boot sector with a partition table for each partition on a disk. If the *adjust partitions to cylinder boundaries* feature is enabled, the **Differ** column should have a value equal to the number of partitions on the source disk because the relocation of each partition requires a change to each partition table. Test cases DI-03, DI-14, and DI-18 had 3 partitions on each source disk.

2. Excess destination sectors (i.e., destination sectors not corresponding to any source sector) are assigned values according to run-time tool options selected by the user. This applies to test cases DI-03, DI-04, DI-07, DI-11, DI-14, DI-18, DI-22, DI-33, DI-53, and DI-54 and test assertions 4, 20, and 27. The content of these sectors is indicated by the columns **Zero Fill, Data Filled,** and **Not Filled**. The expected result is that **Not Filled** is always 0, and the setting of the *zero fill* option determines the expected value of the other two columns. If *zero fill* is enabled, then the expected value for the **Zero Fill** column is **Dst Total—Compared,** and the value of **Data Filled** should be zero. If *zero fill* is not enabled, then the expected value for the **Data Filled** column is **Dst Total—Compared,** and the value of **Zero Fill** should be zero.

3. The tool must notify the user if some source sectors are not copied to the destination. This applies to assertions 5, 11, 17, and 22–26. The **Message** column of the table uses a code to indicate any messages in the tool log file.

   If the source is larger than the destination, then a message should be present in the tool log file indicating that the source is larger than the destination. This applies to test cases DI-02, DI-13, DI-39, DI-40, DI-60, DI-61, and DI-76 and test assertions 5, 11, 17 and 22. The **Message** column should have an **S** to indicate the message is present in the tool log file.

   If there is an I/O error, then there should be a message present in the tool log file indicating that an I/O error has occurred (test assertions *23–26*). The **Message** column should have an **E** to indicate the message is present in the tool log file. This applies to test cases DI-06, DI-07, DI-08, DI-09, DI-11, DI-17, DI-18, DI-22, DI-23, and DI-24.

4. A SafeBack image file contains all the data read from the imaged source plus cyclical redundancy checksums for verifying the integrity of the captured data. The image is divided into blocks of about 119 sectors, and a checksum is computed for each block. The block checksums and a whole-file checksum are appended to the image file. If SafeBack is restoring a source to a destination from an image file, an automatic verification of each block and the whole-file is performed. If an image file is accessed, then the results of an integrity check should be placed in the tool log file (test assertion 32). The **Message** column should have a **V** if the tool log file has a message indicating a checksum verifies message and a **C** if there is a message indicating that the checksum does not verify. This applies to test cases DI-12, DI-14, DI-15, DI-17, DI-18, DI-21, DI-22, DI-24, DI-46, DI-53, DI-54, DI-67, DI-69, DI-70, and DI-71.

5. The source is not changed by the tool (test assertion 28). The tool did not change the source in any of the test cases. This is not indicated in the summary table. A test for this was executed for all test cases. Details are given in the log files for each test case. This was verified by computing a hash of the source before and after testing. If the hashes are the same before and after, then no change was assumed.

6. Using the tool over a communications link yields the same result as would have been obtained without the communications link (test assertion 29). Tests using a communication link are indicated by an **L** in the eighth position of the **Parameters** column. This applies to test cases DI-10, DI-21, DI-32, DI-53, DI-61, and DI-73.

7. Deleted files can be recovered (test assertion 30). This is not indicated in the summary table but applies to test case DI-73. Details are given in the log file for test case DI-73 at the end of this report.

8. The tool does not access areas of the disk outside the boundaries indicated by the BIOS. This applies to test cases DI-75 and DI-76 and test assertion 31. A physical disk may have a different physical geometry from the logical geometry presented by the BIOS. This is because the BIOS interface can only present a disk with less than 1,024 cylinders. If a disk is being accessed by the BIOS and the physical disk contains more than 1,024 cylinders, then the BIOS presents an adjusted (logical) disk geometry with fewer than 1,024 cylinders by increasing the heads per cylinder value and decreasing the number of cylinders value. In a DOS environment, a disk is usually accessed through the BIOS, but software can directly access the physical disk if the necessary device driver is available. For example, the Quantum Sirocco model 1700 has the following direct physical and BIOS access parameters:

Access	Cylinders	Heads	Sectors per Head	Sectors per Cylinder	Total Sectors
Direct	3,309	16	63	1,008	3,335,472
BIOS	826	64	63	4,032	3,330,432

SafeBack Test Results Summary

Case	Parameters	Message	Src Total	Compared	Match	Differ	Lost	Dst Total	Zero Fill	Data Filled	Not Filled	Notes
Di-01	PCBD=-----		3,330,432	3,330,432	3,330,432	0	0	3,330,432	0	0	0	E/r
Di-02	PCB5>-----	S	3,330,432	2,495,808	2,495,808	0	834,624	2,495,808	0	0	0	E/r
Di-03	PCB8<--A---		3,330,432	3,330,432	3,330,423	9	0	12,643,155	41,820	9,269,508	1,395	3,4
Di-04	PCBN<F-----		3,330,432	3,330,432	3,330,432	0	0	12,643,155	9,308,691	4,032	0	4
Di-05	PCB0=-----		30,023,280	30,023,280	30,023,280	0	0	30,023,280	0	0	0	E/r
Di-06	PCBL=----SR	E	3,330,432	3,330,432	3,330,431	1	0	3,330,432	0	0	0	E/r
Di-07	PCBD<FA-DW	E	3,330,432	3,330,432	3,330,423	9	0	12,643,155	9,307,810	4,036	877	3,4
Di-08	PCB0=----SR	E	30,023,280	30,023,280	30,023,279	1	0	30,023,280	0	0	0	E/r
Di-09	PCB0=----DW	E	30,023,280	30,023,280	30,023,247	33	0	30,023,280	0	0	0	E/r
Di-10	PCB5=----L--		3,330,432	3,330,432	3,330,432	0	0	3,330,432	0	0	0	E/r
Di-11	PCB8<--LSR	E	3,330,432	3,330,432	3,330,431	1	0	12,643,155	9,308,691	4,032	0	1,4
Di-12	PIBL=-----	V	3,330,432	3,330,432	3,330,432	0	0	3,330,432	0	0	0	E/r
Di-13	PIBD>-----	S	3,330,432	2,495,808	2,495,808	0	834,624	2,495,808	0	0	0	2
Di-14	PIB5<-A---	V	3,330,432	3,330,432	3,330,423	9	0	12,643,155	26,273	9,285,573	877	3,4
Di-15	PIB8<F-----	V	3,330,432	3,330,432	3,330,432	0	0	12,643,155	9,308,691	4,032	0	4
Di-17	PIBN=----SR	VE	3,330,432	3,330,432	3,330,431	1	0	3,330,432	0	0	0	E/r
Di-18	PIBL<FA-DW	VE	3,334,464	3,334,464	3,334,440	24	0	12,643,155	9,307,939	4	748	3,4
Di-21	PIBD=--L--	V	3,330,432	3,330,432	3,330,432	0	0	3,330,432	0	0	0	E/r
Di-22	PIB5<--LSR	VE	3,330,432	3,330,432	3,330,431	1	0	12,643,155	9,308,691	4,032	0	1,4
Di-23	PIBN=----IW	E										E/r
Di-24	PIB8=----IR	CE	3,330,432	3,330,432	3,330,313	119	0	3,330,432	0	0	0	E/r
Di-25	LCBD=-----		24,129	24,129	24,129	0	0	24,129	0	0	0	E/r
Di-32	LCBD<--L--		44,289	44,289	44,289	0	0	52,353	0	8,064	0	E/r
Di-33	LCB5<-----		104,769	104,769	104,769	0	0	137,025	0	32,256	0	E/r
Di-39	LCBD>-----	S	44,289	40,257	40,257	0	4,032	40,257	0	0	0	E/r
Di-40	LCB5>-----	S	104,769	92,673	92,673	0	12,096	92,673	0	0	0	E/r
Di-46	LIBD=-----	V	44,289	44,289	44,289	0	0	44,289	0	0	0	E/r
Di-53	LIBD<F-L--	V	24,129	24,129	24,129	0	0	28,161	0	4,032	0	E/r
Di-54	LIB5<F-----	V	104,769	104,769	104,769	0	0	145,089	0	40,320	0	E/r
Di-60	LIBD>--L--	S	24,129	20,097	20,097	0	4,032	20,097	0	0	0	2
Di-61	LIB5>--L--	S	104,769	88,641	88,641	0	16,128	88,641	0	0	0	2
Di-67	PVB8<F-----	V										E/r
Di-69	PVB8<F--IC	C										E/r
Di-70	LVB5=-----	V										E/r
Di-71	LVB5=----IC	C										E/r

Case	Parameters	Message	Src Total	Compared	Match	Differ	Lost	Dst Total	Zero Fill	Data Filled	Not Filled	Notes
												SafeBack Test Results Summary
Di-73	PCBD=--L--											E/r
Di-74	PCBN<F-----		3,335,472	3,335,472	3,334,464	1,008	0	12,643,155	9,307,683	0	0	4
Di-75	PCDD=-----		3,335,472	3,335,472	3,335,472	0	0	3,335,472	0	0	0	E/r
Di-76	PCD5>-----	S	3,330,432	2,495,808	2,495,808	0	834,624	2,495,808	0	0	0	E/r
Di-78	PCS-=-----		17,921,835	17,921,835	17,921,835	0	0	17,921,835	0	0	0	E/r
Di-79	PCA-=-----		17,921,835	17,921,835	2,097,270	15,824,565	0	17,921,835	0	0	0	5

9

5.   Results by Test Assertion

This section is a listing by test assertion. The test case number and test results are given for each assertion.

NOTE: Assertion 28 is not included in this listing. Assertion 28 states, *"The source before using the tool must be equal to the source after tool use."* Since not altering the source is fundamental for a forensic tool, the test for this (i.e., hashing the source before and after the actions and comparing the hashes) was run for every test case. Expected results were obtained in every case. The results of these are included in the log files and are generally the next to the last entry. An example of an entry is:

> before = after
> before = 305B31403D8AD36BCB9AF108821818DCFA3F919A
> after = 305B31403D8AD36BCB9AF108821818DCFA3F919A

1.   If a duplicate copy is created directly from a source disk of the same geometry, then the disks must compare equal.
> Di-01   Expected results.
> Di-05   Expected results.
> Di-06   Expected results.
> Di-08   Expected results.
> Di-09   Expected results.
> Di-10   Expected results.
> Di-78   Expected results.

2.   If a duplicate copy is created directly from a source disk of a smaller geometry and cylinder adjustment is enabled, then the disks must compare adjusted equal.
> Di-03   Zero fill done but not requested. Cylinder adjustment anomaly. BIOS anomaly.
> Di-07   Cylinder adjustment anomaly. BIOS anomaly.

3.   If a duplicate copy is created directly from a source disk of a smaller geometry and cylinder adjustment is not enabled, then the disks must compare equal.
> Di-04   BIOS anomaly.
> Di-11   Zero fill done but not requested. BIOS anomaly.

4.   If a duplicate copy is created directly from a source disk of smaller geometry, then the contents of the destination disk sectors not corresponding to source disk sectors must be as specified by the tool (if the tool allows such a specification). Otherwise each bit of such sectors must be set to zero.
> Di-03   Zero fill done but not requested. Cylinder adjustment anomaly. BIOS anomaly.
> Di-04   BIOS anomaly.
> Di-07   Cylinder adjustment anomaly. BIOS anomaly.
> Di-11   Zero fill done but not requested. BIOS anomaly.

5. *If a duplicate copy is created directly from a source disk with the destination disk having a smaller geometry, then the tool must notify the user.*

Di-02 Expected results.

6. *If a duplicate copy is created directly from a source disk with the destination disk having a smaller geometry, then every sector of the destination disk must compare equal to the corresponding sector on the source disk.*

Di-02 Expected results.

7. *If a duplicate destination disk is created from an image file of a source disk with the same geometry, then the disks must compare equal.*

Di-12 Expected results.
Di-17 Expected results.
Di-21 Expected results.
Di-23 Expected results.
Di-24 Expected results.

8. *If a duplicate destination disk is created from an image file of a source disk with a smaller geometry and cylinder adjustment is enabled, then the disks must compare adjusted equal.*

Di-14 Zero fill done but not requested. Cylinder adjustment anomaly. BIOS anomaly.
Di-18 Cylinder adjustment anomaly. BIOS anomaly.

9. *If a duplicate destination disk is created from an image file of a source disk with a smaller geometry and cylinder adjustment is not enabled, then the disks must compare equal.*

Di-15 BIOS anomaly.
Di-22 Zero fill done but not requested. BIOS anomaly.

10. *If a duplicate destination disk is created from an image file of a source disk with a smaller geometry, then the contents of the destination disk sectors not corresponding to source disk sectors must be as specified by the tool (if the tool allows such a specification). Otherwise each bit of such sectors must be set to zero.*

Di-14 Zero fill done but not requested. Cylinder adjustment anomaly. BIOS anomaly.
Di-15 BIOS anomaly.
Di-18 Cylinder adjustment anomaly. BIOS anomaly.
Di-22 Zero fill done but not requested. BIOS anomaly.

11. *If a duplicate destination disk is created from an image file of a source disk with a larger geometry, then the tool must notify the user.*

Di-13 Checksum verify message missing.

12. *If a duplicate destination disk is created from an image file of a source disk with a larger geometry, then every sector of the destination disk must compare equal to the corresponding sector on the source disk.*

Di-13 Checksum verify message missing.

13. *If a duplicate destination partition is created directly from a source partition of the same size, then each sector of the source partition must compare equal to the logical block address (LBA) corresponding sector of the destination partition.*
Di-25 Expected results.

14. *If a duplicate destination partition is created directly from a smaller source partition, then each sector of the source partition must compare equal to the LBA corresponding sector of the destination partition.*
Di-32 Expected results.
Di-33 Expected results.

15. *If a duplicate destination partition is created directly from a smaller source partition, then each sector of the destination partition with no LBA corresponding sector in the source partition must be as specified by the tool (if the tool allows such a specification). Otherwise each bit of each sector must be set to zero.*
Di-32 Expected results.
Di-33 Expected results.

16. *If a duplicate destination partition is created directly from a larger source partition, then each sector of the destination partition must compare equal to the LBA corresponding sector of the source partition.*
Di-39 Expected results.
Di-40 Expected results.

17. *If a duplicate destination partition is created directly from a larger source partition, then the tool must notify the user.*
Di-39 Expected results.
Di-40 Expected results.

18. *If a duplicate destination partition is created from an image file of a source partition of the same size, then each sector of the source partition must compare equal to the LBA corresponding sector of the destination partition.*
Di-46 Expected results.

19. *If a duplicate destination partition is created from an image file of a smaller source partition, then each sector of the source partition must compare equal to the LBA corresponding sector of the destination partition.*
Di-53 Expected results.
Di-54 Expected results.

20. *If a duplicate destination partition is created from an image file of a smaller source partition, then each sector of the destination partition with no LBA corresponding sector in the source partition must be as specified by the tool (if the tool allows such a specification). Otherwise each bit of each sector must be set to zero.*
Di-53 Expected results.
Di-54 Expected results.

21. *If a duplicate destination partition is created from an image file of a larger source partition, then each sector of the destination partition must compare equal to the LBA corresponding sector of the source partition.*

      Di-60 Checksum verify message missing.
      Di-61 Checksum verify message missing.

22. *If a duplicate destination partition is created from an image file of a larger source partition, then the tool must notify the user.*

      Di-60 Checksum verify message missing.
      Di-61 Checksum verify message missing.

23. *If the tool encounters any read errors while reading from the source, then the tool must detect and identify the error and notify the user.*

      Di-06 Expected results.
      Di-08 Expected results.
      Di-11 Zero fill done but not requested. BIOS anomaly.
      Di-17 Expected results.
      Di-22 Zero fill done but not requested. BIOS anomaly.

24. *If the tool encounters any read errors while reading from an image file, then the tool must detect and identify the error and notify the user.*

      Di-24 Expected results.

25. *If the tool encounters any write errors while creating an image file, then the tool must detect and identify the error and notify the user.*

      Di-23 Expected results.

26. *If the tool encounters any write errors while writing to the destination, then the tool must detect and identify the error and notify the user.*

      Di-07 Cylinder adjustment anomaly. BIOS anomaly.
      Di-09 Expected results.
      Di-18 Cylinder adjustment anomaly. BIOS anomaly.

27. *If the tool is able to create a destination from an image file that contains read errors, the destination sectors corresponding to the unreadable data must be treated as fill sectors (the tool may allow a specified action or may fill the sectors with zeros).*

      Di-06 Expected results.
      Di-08 Expected results.
      Di-11 Zero fill done but not requested. BIOS anomaly.
      Di-17 Expected results.
      Di-22 Zero fill done but not requested. BIOS anomaly.
      Di-24 Expected results.
      Di-69 Expected results.
      Di-71 Expected results.

29. *The results of any remote tool use must be equal to the results of local identical tool use.*

    Di-10 Expected results.
    Di-11 Zero fill done but not requested. BIOS anomaly.
    Di-22 Zero fill done but not requested. BIOS anomaly.
    Di-32 Expected results.
    Di-53 Expected results.
    Di-61 Checksum verify message missing.
    Di-73 Expected results.

30. *If deleted files exist that are recoverable on the source, then these files must be recoverable on the destination.*

    Di-73 Expected results.

31. *If the logical disk as presented by the BIOS is smaller than the physical disk, then the tool must not access any sectors outside the logical disk.*

    Di-74 BIOS anomaly.

32. *If the tool has a feature to verify the integrity of the image file, the tool shall detect and identify the anomaly and notify the user if the image file has been changed.*

    Di-67 Expected results.
    Di-69 Expected results.
    Di-70 Expected results.
    Di-71 Expected results.

33. *If a duplicate copy is created directly, without using the BIOS, from a source disk of the same geometry, then the disks must compare equal.*

    Di-75 Expected results.
    Di-79 Expected results.

34. *If a duplicate copy is created directly, without using the BIOS, from a source disk of a smaller geometry and cylinder adjustment is enabled, then the disks must compare adjusted equal. No test cases apply.*

35. *If a duplicate copy is created directly, without using the BIOS, from a source disk with the destination disk having a smaller geometry, then the tool must notify the user.*

    Di-76 Expected results.

6.   Summary Log Files

Test case ID DI-01

Test assertions

1.   If a duplicate copy is created directly from a source disk of the same geometry, then the disks must compare equal.

28.   The source before using the tool must be equal to the source after tool use.

   Setup

1. wipe(src)
```
A:\DISKWIPE.EXE @(#) Version 2.1 Created 09/27/00 at 13:44:51
Comment: DOS Setup
run start Wed Sep 27 17:47:09 2000
run finish Wed Sep 27 17:54:19 2000
drive 0x80 (master) no BIOS extensions
3330432 sectors wiped with D1
```
2. partition(src,1,*,Fat 12)
3. partition(src,2,*,Small Fat 16)
4. load_os(DOS)
```
Comment: beta5 D1 (DOS) Layout
Source disk partition table
P 000000063 000024129 0000/001/01 0005/063/63 Boot 01 Fat12
X 000024192 003306240 0006/000/01 0825/063/63       05 extended
S 000000063 000044289 0006/001/01 0016/063/63       04 Fat16
x 000044352 003261888 0017/000/01 0825/063/63       05 extended
S 000000063 003261825 0017/001/01 0825/063/63       06 Fat16
Source disk layout:  00826/064/63 3330432 total sectors on disk
        Start LBA    End LBA    Length    Size: MB    (binary)
 0 B          0         62        63     0.03MB      0.03BMB
 1 P         63      24191     24129    12.35MB     11.78BMB
 2 b      24192      24254        63     0.03MB      0.03BMB
 3 P      24255      68543     44289    22.68MB     21.63BMB
 4 b      68544      68606        63     0.03MB      0.03BMB
 5 P      68607    3330431   3261825  1670.05MB   1592.69BMB
```

5. before=hash(src)
```
A:\DISKHASH.EXE @(#) Version 2.1 Created 09/27/00 at 13:44:51
Comment: hash D1 before running SafeBack
run start Fri Sep 29 11:06:09 2000
run finish Fri Sep 29 12:09:44 2000
drive 0x80 (master) no BIOS extensions
Disk SHA-1 hash 305B31403D8AD36BCB9AF108821818DCFA3F919A
```
6. wipe(dst)
```
A:\DISKWIPE.EXE @(#) Version 2.1 Created 09/27/00 at 13:44:51
Comment:
run start Thu Sep 28 11:15:31 2000
run finish Thu Sep 28 11:22:27 2000
drive 0x80 (master) no BIOS extensions
3330432 sectors wiped with D2
```
   Execute

7. copy(src,dst)
```
        SafeBack 2.0 31Jan00 execution started on Sep 29, 2000 12:15.
```

15

```
12:16:10   Menu selections:
               Function:              Copy
               Remote connection:     Local
               Direct access:         No
               Use XBIOS:             Auto
               Adjust partitions:     Auto
               Backfill on restore:   Yes
               Compress sector data:  Yes
12:16:29   Copy from Local drive 0: to local drive 1:
12:16:53   Copy of Local drive 0: to drive 1: begun on Sep 29, 2000 12:16
12:16:53   Local SafeBack is running on DOS 6.30
12:16:53   Partition table for drive 0:
           Source drive 0:
               Capacity.......1628 MB
               Cylinders.......827
               Heads..........64
           Destination drive 1:
               Capacity.......1628 MB
               Cylinders......827
               Heads..........64
12:25:37   Partition table for drive 1:
12:25:38   Copy of drive 0: to drive 1: completed on Sep 29, 2000 12:25
```
   Measure

8. after=hash(src)
```
A:\DISKHASH.EXE @(#) Version 2.1 Created 09/27/00 at 13:44:51
Comment: Hash D1 after SafeBack
run start Fri Sep 29 13:04:41 2000
run finish Fri Sep 29 14:07:25 2000
drive 0x80 (master) no BIOS extensions
Disk SHA-1 hash 305B31403D8AD36BCB9AF108821818DCFA3F919A
```

9. Compare(src,dst)
```
Comment: Test DI-01 on beta1
run start Fri Sep 29 12:37:26 2000
run finish Fri Sep 29 12:48:55 2000
sectors compared 3330432 match 3330432 differ 0 dropped 0
filled: zero 0 src 0 dst 0 other 0 remainder 0
```
   Output Specifications (expected results)

10. before=after
```
before = 305B31403D8AD36BCB9AF108821818DCFA3F919A
after  = 305B31403D8AD36BCB9AF108821818DCFA3F919A
```
11. src and dst compare equal
```
sectors compared 3330432 match 3330432 differ 0 dropped 0
```

Test case ID DI-02

Test assertions

5.   If a duplicate copy is created directly from a source disk with the destination disk having a smaller geometry, then the tool must notify the user.

6.   If a duplicate copy is created directly from a source disk with the destination disk having a smaller geometry, then every sector of the destination disk must compare equal to the corresponding sector on the source disk.

28.   The source before using the tool must be equal to the source after tool use.

   Setup

1. wipe(src)
```
A:\DISKWIPE.EXE @(#) Version 2.1 Created 09/27/00 at 13:44:51
```

```
Comment: Windows 95 setup
run start Wed Sep 27 17:52:35 2000
run finish Wed Sep 27 17:59:47 2000
drive 0x80 (master) no BIOS extensions
3330432 sectors wiped with F1
```

2. partition(src,1,*,Big Fat 16)

3. load_os(Windows 95)

```
Comment: beta5 F1 W95 layout
Source disk partition table
P 000000063 003072321 0000/001/01 0761/063/63 Boot 06 Fat16
X 003072384 000258048 0762/000/01 0825/063/63      05 extended
S 000000063 000104769 0762/001/01 0787/063/63      06 Fat16
x 000104832 000153216 0788/000/01 0825/063/63      05 extended
S 000000063 000153153 0788/001/01 0825/063/63      06 Fat16
Source disk layout:  00826/064/63 3330432 total sectors on disk
      Start LBA    End LBA    Length    Size: MB   (binary)
   0 B         0        62        63     0.03MB     0.03BMB
   1 P        63   3072383   3072321  1573.03MB  1500.16BMB
   2 b   3072384   3072446        63     0.03MB     0.03BMB
   3 P   3072447   3177215    104769    53.64MB    51.16BMB
   4 b   3177216   3177278        63     0.03MB     0.03BMB
   5 P   3177279   3330431    153153    78.41MB    74.78BMB
```

4. before=hash(src)

```
A:\DISKHASH.EXE @(#) Version 2.2 Created 10/02/00 at 09:08:26
Comment: rehash F1 (Win 95)
run start Fri Nov 03 14:08:19 2000
run finish Fri Nov 03 14:28:46 2000
drive 0x80 (master) no BIOS extensions
Disk SHA-1 hash 5FBEEB219E7282ED621645A67252A70F4D8BBF21
```

5. wipe(dst)

```
A:\DISKWIPE.EXE @(#) Version 2.1 Created 09/27/00 at 13:44:51
Comment: beta5 DI-02
run start Tue Nov 28 11:17:39 2000
run finish Tue Nov 28 11:32:12 2000
drive 0x80 (master) no BIOS extensions
2495808 sectors wiped with D5
```

Execute

6. copy(src,dst)

```
          SafeBack 2.0 31Jan00 execution started on Nov 28, 2000 11:38.
11:38:43  Menu selections:
              Function:            Copy
              Remote connection:   Local
              Direct access:       No
              Use XBIOS:           Auto
              Adjust partitions:   Auto
              Backfill on restore: Yes
              Compress sector data: Yes
11:38:53  Copy from Local drive 1: to local drive 0:
11:38:53  Insufficient destination file space projected.
11:39:07  Copy of Local drive 1: to drive 0: begun on Nov 28, 2000 11:39
11:39:07  Local SafeBack is running on DOS 6.30
11:39:07  Partition table for drive 1:
          Source drive 1:
             Capacity........1628 MB
             Cylinders.......827
             Heads..........64
          Destination drive 0:
```

```
              Capacity........1221 MB
              Cylinders.......620
              Heads..........64
11:59:56  Partition table for drive 0:
11:59:56  Copy of drive 1: to drive 0: completed on Nov 28, 2000 11:59
          SafeBack execution ended on Nov 28, 2000 12:00.
```

Measure

7. after=hash(src)
```
A:\DISKHASH.EXE %Z% Version %I% Created %G% at %U%
Comment: beta5 hash F1 after DI-02,14,33,40,54,61
run start Tue Nov 28 15:03:27 2000
run finish Tue Nov 28 15:24:20 2000
drive 0x80 (master) no BIOS extensions
Disk SHA-1 hash 5FBEEB219E7282ED621645A67252A70F4D8BBF21
```

8. Examine_message(Destination too small)
```
11:38:53  Insufficient destination file space projected.
```

9. Compare(src,dst)
```
Comment: Beta2 DI-02 F1->D5
run start Tue Nov 28 12:00:41 2000
run finish Tue Nov 28 12:11:21 2000
sectors compared 2495808 match 2495808 differ 0 dropped 834624
filled: zero 0 src 0 dst 0 other 0 remainder 0
```

Output Specifications (expected results)

10. before=after
```
before = 5FBEEB219E7282ED621645A67252A70F4D8BBF21
after  = 5FBEEB219E7282ED621645A67252A70F4D8BBF21
```

11. Destination too small message
```
11:38:53  Insufficient destination file space projected.
```

12. src and dst compare equal
```
sectors compared 2495808 match 2495808 differ 0 dropped 834624
```

Test case ID DI-03

Test assertions

2.   If a duplicate copy is created directly from a source disk of a smaller geometry and cylinder adjustment is enabled, then the disks must compare adjusted equal.
4.   If a duplicate copy is created directly from a source disk of smaller geometry, then the contents of the destination disk sectors not corresponding to source disk sectors must be as specified by the tool (if the tool allows such a specification). Otherwise each bit of such sectors must be set to zero.
28.   The source before using the tool must be equal to the source after tool use.

Setup

1. wipe(src)
```
A:\DISKWIPE.EXE @(#) Version 2.1 Created 09/27/00 at 13:44:51
Comment: Windows 98 setup
run start Wed Sep 27 17:40:45 2000
run finish Wed Sep 27 17:48:08 2000
drive 0x80 (master) no BIOS extensions
3330432 sectors wiped with F2
```

2. partition(src,1,*,Fat 32)

3. load_os(Windows 98)
```
Comment: beta5 F2 (W98) layout
Source disk partition table
P 000000063 001640961 0000/001/01 0406/063/63 Boot 0B Fat32
```

```
X 001641024 001689408 0407/000/01 0825/063/63      05 extended
S 000000063 001640961 0407/001/01 0813/063/63      0B Fat32
x 001641024 000048384 0814/000/01 0825/063/63      05 extended
S 000000063 000048321 0814/001/01 0825/063/63      04 Fat16
Source disk layout:  00826/064/63 3330432 total sectors on disk
        Start LBA    End LBA    Length    Size: MB   (binary)
  0 B          0         62         63     0.03MB    0.03BMB
  1 P         63    1641023    1640961   840.17MB  801.25BMB
  2 b    1641024    1641086         63     0.03MB    0.03BMB
  3 P    1641087    3282047    1640961   840.17MB  801.25BMB
  4 b    3282048    3282110         63     0.03MB    0.03BMB
  5 P    3282111    3330431      48321    24.74MB   23.59BMB
```

4. before=hash(src)

```
A:\DISKHASH.EXE @(#) Version 2.1 Created 09/27/00 at 13:44:51
Comment: reference hash for F2
run start Fri Sep 29 11:46:04 2000
run finish Fri Sep 29 12:49:43 2000
drive 0x80 (master) no BIOS extensions
Disk SHA-1 hash 96EDE9BC7D9A33A61A5537C5CB7DF45CAD6ED488
```

5. wipe(dst)

```
A:\DISKWIPE.EXE @(#) Version 2.2 Created 10/02/00 at 09:08:26
Comment: beta5 wipe D11 for DI-03
run start Sat Nov 18 13:35:13 2000
run finish Sat Nov 18 13:47:44 2000
drive 0x80 (master) no BIOS extensions
12643155 sectors wiped with DB
```

  Execute

6. copy(src,dst,n,a)

```
           SafeBack 2.0 31Jan00 execution started on Nov 18, 2000 13:26.
13:26:52  Menu selections:
              Function:              Copy
              Remote connection:     Local
              Direct access:         No
              Use XBIOS:             Auto
              Adjust partitions:     Auto
              Backfill on restore:   No
              Compress sector data:  Yes
13:27:04  Copy from Local drive 0: to local drive 1:
13:27:14  Copy of Local drive 0: to drive 1: begun on Nov 18, 2000 13:27
13:27:14  Local SafeBack is running on DOS 6.30
13:27:14  Partition table for drive 0:
          Source drive 0:
              Capacity........1628 MB
              Cylinders.......827
              Heads..........64
          Destination drive 1:
              Capacity........6181 MB
              Cylinders.......788
              Heads..........255
13:27:14  Boot sector located at relative sector 63 (Cylinder 0, Head 1, Sector
1)
13:31:09  Boot sector located at relative sector 1654758 (Cylinder 103, Head 1,
Sector 1)
13:35:05  Boot sector located at relative sector 3309453 (Cylinder 206, Head 1,
Sector 1)
13:35:16  Partition table for drive 1:
```

```
13:35:17  Copy of drive 0: to drive 1: completed on Nov 18, 2000 13:35
          SafeBack execution ended on Nov 18, 2000 13:36.
```
   Measure
7. after=hash(src)
```
A:\DISKHASH.EXE @(#) Version 2.2 Created 10/02/00 at 09:08:26
Comment: beta5 hash F2 after DI-03
run start Sat Nov 18 15:18:39 2000
run finish Sat Nov 18 15:38:57 2000
drive 0x80 (master) no BIOS extensions
Disk SHA-1 hash 96EDE9BC7D9A33A61A5537C5CB7DF45CAD6ED488
```
8. Compare(src,dst)
```
A:\ADJCMP.EXE @(#) Version 2.1 Created 10/10/00 at 15:36:36
Comment: Beta4 DI-03 F2=>D11 no fill adjust PT
run start Sat Nov 18 13:39:05 2000
run finish Sat Nov 18 14:14:07 2000
3 partitions, Boot track sectors: compared 189 match 186 differ 3
Data track sectors: compared 3330243 match 3330237 differ 6
Data track sectors filled: zero 41820 src 3 dst 9265473 other 4032 remaining
1395
```
   Output Specifications (expected results)
9. before=after
```
before = 96EDE9BC7D9A33A61A5537C5CB7DF45CAD6ED488
after  = 96EDE9BC7D9A33A61A5537C5CB7DF45CAD6ED488
```
10. src and dst compare adjusted equal
```
3 partitions, Boot track sectors: compared 189 match 186 differ 3
Data track sectors: compared 3330243 match 3330237 differ 6
```

Test case ID DI-04

Test assertions

3.   If a duplicate copy is created directly from a source disk of a smaller geometry and cylinder adjustment is not enabled, then the disks must compare equal.

4.   If a duplicate copy is created directly from a source disk of smaller geometry, then the contents of the destination disk sectors not corresponding to source disk sectors must be as specified by the tool (if the tool allows such a specification). Otherwise each bit of such sectors must be set to zero.

28.   The source before using the tool must be equal to the source after tool use.

   Setup

1. wipe(src)
```
A:\DISKWIPE.EXE @(#) Version 2.1 Created 09/27/00 at 13:44:51
Comment: initial setup for NT
run start Wed Sep 27 14:37:32 2000
run finish Wed Sep 27 14:44:44 2000
drive 0x80 (master) no BIOS extensions
3330432 sectors wiped with D9
```
2. partition(src,1,*,NTFS)

3. load_os(Windows NT)
```
Comment: beta5 D9 (NT) layout
Source disk partition table
P 000000063 003072321 0000/001/01 0761/063/63 Boot 07 NTFS
X 003072384 000262080 0762/000/01 0826/063/63      05 extended
S 000000063 000060417 0762/001/01 0776/063/63      07 NTFS
x 000060480 000080640 0777/000/01 0796/063/63      05 extended
S 000000063 000080577 0777/001/01 0796/063/63      07 NTFS
```

20

```
x 000141120 000120960 0797/000/01 0826/063/63      05 extended
S 000000063 000120897 0797/001/01 0826/063/63      07 NTFS
Source disk layout: 00826/064/63 3330432 total sectors on disk
       Start LBA    End LBA    Length   Size: MB   (binary)
  0 B          0         62        63    0.03MB    0.03BMB
  1 P         63    3072383   3072321 1573.03MB 1500.16BMB
  2 b    3072384    3072446        63    0.03MB    0.03BMB
  3 P    3072447    3132863     60417   30.93MB   29.50BMB
  4 b    3132864    3132926        63    0.03MB    0.03BMB
  5 P    3132927    3213503     80577   41.26MB   39.34BMB
  6 b    3213504    3213566        63    0.03MB    0.03BMB
  7 P    3213567    3334463    120897   61.90MB   59.03BMB
```

4. before=hash(src)

```
A:\DISKHASH.EXE @(#) Version 2.1 Created 09/27/00 at 13:44:51
Comment: Reference hash on D9 (NTFS)
run start Fri Sep 29 11:21:28 2000
run finish Fri Sep 29 12:26:11 2000
drive 0x80 (master) no BIOS extensions
Disk SHA-1 hash A683672031589F08895F3AEDE8DBC77718648284
```

5. wipe(dst)

```
A:\DISKWIPE.EXE @(#) Version 2.2 Created 10/02/00 at 09:08:26
Comment: beta5 DI-04 wipe D11
run start Mon Nov 20 16:06:19 2000
run finish Mon Nov 20 16:17:37 2000
drive 0x80 (master) no BIOS extensions
12643155 sectors wiped with DB
```

Execute

6. copy(src,dst,f,n)

```
          SafeBack 2.0 31Jan00 execution started on Nov 20, 2000 16:23.
16:23:39  Menu selections:
              Function:             Copy
              Remote connection:    Local
              Direct access:        No
              Use XBIOS:            Auto
              Adjust partitions:    No
              Backfill on restore:  Yes
              Compress sector data: Yes
16:23:46  Copy from Local drive 0: to local drive 1:
16:23:58  Copy of Local drive 0: to drive 1: begun on Nov 20, 2000 16:23
16:23:58  Local SafeBack is running on DOS 6.30
16:23:58  Partition table for drive 0:
          Source drive 0:
              Capacity........1628 MB
              Cylinders.......827
              Heads...........64
          Destination drive 1:
              Capacity........6181 MB
              Cylinders.......788
              Heads...........255
16:39:21  Copy of drive 0: to drive 1: completed on Nov 20, 2000 16:39
          SafeBack execution ended on Nov 20, 2000 16:40.
```

Measure

7. after=hash(src)

```
A:\DISKHASH.EXE @(#) Version 2.2 Created 10/02/00 at 09:08:26
Comment: hash D9 after DI-04 on beta5
run start Mon Nov 20 17:20:39 2000
run finish Mon Nov 20 17:41:34 2000
```

```
drive 0x80 (master) no BIOS extensions
Disk SHA-1 hash A683672031589F08895F3AEDE8DBC77718648284
```

8. Compare(src,dst)

```
Comment: beta4 DI-04
run start Mon Nov 20 16:45:25 2000
run finish Mon Nov 20 17:14:57 2000
sectors compared 3330432 match 3330432 differ 0 dropped 0
filled: zero 9308691 src 0  dst 0  other 4032 remainder 0
```

   Output Specifications (expected results)

9. before=after

```
before = A683672031589F08895F3AEDE8DBC77718648284
after  = A683672031589F08895F3AEDE8DBC77718648284
```

10. src and dst compare equal

```
sectors compared 3330432 match 3330432 differ 0 dropped 0
```

11. excess dst sectors zero filled

```
filled: zero 9308691 src 0  dst 0  other 4032 remainder 0
```

Test case ID DI-05

Test assertions

1.   *If a duplicate copy is created directly from a source disk of the same geometry, then the disks must compare equal.*

28.   *The source before using the tool must be equal to the source after tool use.*

   Setup

1. wipe(src)

```
A:\DISKWIPE.EXE @(#) Version 2.1 Created 09/27/00 at 13:44:51
Comment: wipeout slave drive
run start Fri Sep 29 07:53:59 2000
run finish Fri Sep 29 08:18:29 2000
drive 0x81 (slave) use BIOS extensions
30023280 sectors wiped with B1
```

2. partition(src,1,*,NTFS)

3. partition(src,2,*,Fat 32)

4. load_os(Windows 2000)

```
Comment: beta5 B1 W2000 layout
src B0 dst B1
Source disk partition table
P 000000063 004096512 0000/001/01 0254/254/63      07 NTFS
P 004096575 000048195 0255/000/01 0257/254/63      04 Fat16
P 004144770 000096390 0258/000/01 0263/254/63      06 Fat16
X 004241160 025768260 0264/000/01 1023/254/63      0F extended
S 000000063 000016002 0264/001/01 0264/254/63      01 Fat12
x 000016065 000096390 0265/000/01 0270/254/63      05 extended
S 000000063 000096327 0265/001/01 0270/254/63      06 Fat16
x 000112455 002040255 0271/000/01 0397/254/63      05 extended
S 000000063 002040192 0271/001/01 0397/254/63      06 Fat16
x 002152710 002040255 0398/000/01 0524/254/63      05 extended
S 000000063 002040192 0398/001/01 0524/254/63      0B Fat32
x 004192965 021575295 0525/000/01 1023/254/63      05 extended
S 000000063 021575232 0525/001/01 1023/254/63      07 NTFS
Source disk layout:  01023/255/63 16434495 total sectors on disk
      Start LBA    End LBA    Length    Size: MB    (binary)
  0 B         0         62        63     0.03MB     0.03BMB
  1 P        63    4096574   4096512  2097.41MB  2000.25BMB
  2 P   4096575    4144769     48195    24.68MB    23.53BMB
```

22

```
 3 P    4144770    4241159      96390    49.35MB    47.07BMB
 4 b    4241160    4241222         63     0.03MB     0.03BMB
 5 P    4241223    4257224      16002     8.19MB     7.81BMB
 6 b    4257225    4257287         63     0.03MB     0.03BMB
 7 P    4257288    4353614      96327    49.32MB    47.03BMB
 8 b    4353615    4353677         63     0.03MB     0.03BMB
 9 P    4353678    6393869    2040192  1044.58MB   996.19BMB
10 b    6393870    6393932         63     0.03MB     0.03BMB
11 P    6393933    8434124    2040192  1044.58MB   996.19BMB
12 b    8434125    8434187         63     0.03MB     0.03BMB
13 P    8434188   30009419   21575232 11046.52MB 10534.78BMB
```

5. before=hash(src)

```
A:\DISKHASH.EXE @(#) Version 2.1 Created 09/27/00 at 13:44:51
Comment: Hashing slave (src) before running SafeBack
run start Fri Sep 29 11:16:56 2000
run finish Fri Sep 29 12:44:30 2000
drive 0x81 (slave) use BIOS extensions
Disk SHA-1 hash BB9F63C7247DA70B8C8812AE1EDC1FB58FB9FD98
```

6. wipe(dst)

```
A:\DISKWIPE.EXE @(#) Version 2.1 Created 09/27/00 at 13:44:51
Comment: Setup for windows 2000 on beta5
run start Thu Sep 28 16:00:38 2000
run finish Thu Sep 28 16:14:16 2000
drive 0x80 (master) no BIOS extensions
16434495 sectors wiped with B0
```

Execute

7. copy(src,dst)

```
          SafeBack 2.0 31Jan00 execution started on Sep 29, 2000 13:15.
13:15:59  Menu selections:
              Function:              Copy
              Remote connection:     Local
              Direct access:         No
              Use XBIOS:             Auto
              Adjust partitions:     Auto
              Backfill on restore:   Yes
              Compress sector data:  Yes
13:16:20  Copy from Local drive 1: to local drive 0:
13:16:30  Partition/Boot information saved to A:\PT-DI05.SPS.
13:16:31  Copy of Local drive 1: to drive 0: begun on Sep 29, 2000 13:16
13:16:31  Local SafeBack is running on DOS 6.30
13:16:31  Partition table for drive 1:
          Source drive 1:
              Capacity........14660 MB
              Cylinders.......1868
              Heads...........255
          Destination drive 0:
              Capacity........14660 MB
              Cylinders.......1868
              Heads...........255
13:51:53  Partition table for drive 0:
13:51:54  Copy of drive 1: to drive 0: completed on Sep 29, 2000 13:51
          SafeBack execution ended on Sep 29, 2000 15:16.
```

Measure

8. after=hash(src)

```
A:\DISKHASH.EXE @(#) Version 2.2 Created 10/02/00 at 09:08:26
Comment: test DI-05, beta5, after running SafeBack
run start Mon Oct 02 09:20:52 2000
```

```
run finish Mon Oct 02 10:48:21 2000
drive 0x81 (slave) use BIOS extensions
Disk SHA-1 hash BB9F63C7247DA70B8C8812AE1EDC1FB58FB9FD98
```
9. Compare(src,dst)
```
Comment: beta5, test DI-05
run start Mon Oct 02 08:21:59 2000
run finish Mon Oct 02 08:56:44 2000
sectors compared 30023280 match 30023280 differ 0 dropped 0
filled: zero 0 src 0 dst 0 other 0 remainder 0
```
   Output Specifications (expected results)
10. before=after
```
before = BB9F63C7247DA70B8C8812AE1EDC1FB58FB9FD98
after  = BB9F63C7247DA70B8C8812AE1EDC1FB58FB9FD98
```
11. src and dst compare equal
```
sectors compared 30023280 match 30023280 differ 0 dropped 0
```

Test case ID DI-06

Test assertions

1.   If a duplicate copy is created directly from a source disk of the same geometry, then the disks must compare equal.

23.   If the tool encounters any read errors while reading from the source, then the tool must detect and identify the error and notify the user.

27.   If the tool is able to create a destination from an image file that contains read errors, the destination sectors corresponding to the unreadable data must be treated as fill sectors (the tool may allow a specified action or may fill the sectors with zeros).

28.   The source before using the tool must be equal to the source after tool use.

   Setup

1. wipe(src)
```
A:\DISKWIPE.EXE @(#) Version 2.1 Created 09/27/00 at 13:44:51
Comment: Linux setup
run start Thu Sep 28 14:49:16 2000
run finish Thu Sep 28 14:56:29 2000
drive 0x80 (master) no BIOS extensions
3330432 sectors wiped with D4
```
2. partition(src,1,*,Linux)
3. partition(src,2,*,Linux Swap)
4. load_os(Linux)
```
Comment: D4 (linux) layout
Source disk partition table
P 000000063 002048193 0000/001/01 0507/063/63 Boot 83 Linux
X 002048256 001286208 0508/000/01 0826/063/63      05 extended
S 000000063 000205569 0508/001/01 0558/063/63      82 Linux swap
x 000205632 001080576 0559/000/01 0826/063/63      05 extended
S 000000063 001080513 0559/001/01 0826/063/63      83 Linux
Source disk layout:  00826/064/63 3330432 total sectors on disk
      Start LBA   End LBA    Length    Size: MB   (binary)
  0 B         0        62        63     0.03MB     0.03BMB
  1 P        63   2048255   2048193  1048.67MB  1000.09BMB
  2 b   2048256   2048318        63     0.03MB     0.03BMB
  3 P   2048319   2253887    205569   105.25MB   100.38BMB
  4 b   2253888   2253950        63     0.03MB     0.03BMB
  5 P   2253951   3334463   1080513   553.22MB   527.59BMB
```

5. before=hash(src)

```
A:\DISKHASH.EXE @(#) Version 2.2 Created 10/02/00 at 09:08:26
Comment: beta5, hash d4 for test DI-12
run start Thu Oct 12 08:39:28 2000
run finish Thu Oct 12 08:59:54 2000
drive 0x80 (master) no BIOS extensions
Disk SHA-1 hash D25C035B74F3EECFCBA4A1968AA6D48096D92EE2
```

6. wipe(dst)

```
A:\DISKWIPE.EXE @(#) Version 2.2 Created 10/02/00 at 09:08:26
Comment: beta5 wipe D2
run start Mon Nov 13 11:35:08 2000
run finish Mon Nov 13 11:42:16 2000
drive 0x80 (master) no BIOS extensions
3330432 sectors wiped with D2
```

Execute

7. baddisk(src,read)

```
return code 00010 on command 00002 from disk 00128 (00063 Max head value)
at address 00037/00017/00028
baddisk   compiled on 11/03/00 at 09:12:12
@(#) Version 1.1 Created 11/03/00 at 09:11:04
return code 00010 on command 00010 from disk 00128 (00063 Max head value)
at address 00037/00017/00028
baddisk   compiled on 11/03/00 at 09:12:12
@(#) Version 1.1 Created 11/03/00 at 09:11:04
```

8. copy(src,dst)

```
          SafeBack 2.0 31Jan00 execution started on Nov 13, 2000 11:58.
11:58:09  Menu selections:
              Function:              Copy
              Remote connection:     Local
              Direct access:         No
              Use XBIOS:             Auto
              Adjust partitions:     Auto
              Backfill on restore:   Yes
              Compress sector data:  Yes
11:58:15  Copy from Local drive 0: to local drive 1:
11:58:25  Copy of Local drive 0: to drive 1: begun on Nov 13, 2000 11:58
11:58:25  Local SafeBack is running on DOS 6.30
11:58:25  Partition table for drive 0:
          Source drive 0:
             Capacity........1628 MB
             Cylinders.......827
             Heads...........64
          Destination drive 1:
             Capacity........1628 MB
             Cylinders.......827
             Heads...........64
11:58:50  While reading drive 0: a sector flagged bad error (status 0a)
occurred:
          at relative sector 150282 (Cylinder 37, Head 17, Sector 28)
12:07:30  Partition table for drive 1:
12:07:30  Copy of drive 0: to drive 1: completed on Nov 13, 2000 12:07
          SafeBack execution ended on Nov 13, 2000 12:09.
```

Measure

9. after=hash(src)

```
A:\DISKHASH.EXE @(#) Version 2.2 Created 10/02/00 at 09:08:26
Comment: beta5 hash D4 after test DI-06
```

```
run start Mon Nov 13 12:31:53 2000
run finish Mon Nov 13 12:52:19 2000
drive 0x80 (master) no BIOS extensions
Disk SHA-1 hash D25C035B74F3EECFCBA4A1968AA6D48096D92EE2
```
10. Examine_message(I/O error)
```
11:58:50  While reading drive 0: a sector flagged bad error (status 0a)
occurred:
```
11. Compare(src,dst)
```
Comment: beta3 DI-06 D4==>D2 read error 10 (0Ah) at 37/17/28
run start Mon Nov 13 12:13:35 2000
run finish Mon Nov 13 12:25:25 2000
sectors compared 3330432 match 3330431 differ 1 dropped 0
filled: zero 0 src 0 dst 0 other 0 remainder 0
```
Output Specifications (expected results)
12. before=after
```
before = D25C035B74F3EECFCBA4A1968AA6D48096D92EE2
after  = D25C035B74F3EECFCBA4A1968AA6D48096D92EE2
```
13. I/O error message
```
11:58:50  While reading drive 0: a sector flagged bad error (status 0a)
occurred:
```
14. src and dst compare qualified equal
```
sectors compared 3330432 match 3330431 differ 1 dropped 0
```

Note: Two disks *compare qualified equal* if there exists at least one *non-comparable region* (defined below) and if ignoring sectors in all non-comparable regions, the disks compare equal or adjusted equal as appropriate.

A *non-comparable region* is a contiguous set of corresponding sectors that contains at least one *non-comparable sector pair.*

A *non-comparable sector pair* is a pair of corresponding sectors if at least one of the following is true:
1. The source sector cannot be read.
2. The destination sector cannot be written.
3. At least one byte from the source sector is contained in a sector that cannot be read of an image file created from the source and used to create the destination.

Test case ID DI-07

Test assertions
2.   If a duplicate copy is created directly from a source disk of a smaller geometry and cylinder adjustment is enabled, then the disks must compare adjusted equal.
4.   If a duplicate copy is created directly from a source disk of smaller geometry, then the contents of the destination disk sectors not corresponding to source disk sectors must be as specified by the tool (if the tool allows such a specification). Otherwise each bit of such sectors must be set to zero.
26.   If the tool encounters any write errors while writing to the destination, then the tool must detect and identify the error and notify the user.
28.   The source before using the tool must be equal to the source after tool use.

Setup

1. wipe(src)

```
A:\DISKWIPE.EXE @(#) Version 2.1 Created 09/27/00 at 13:44:51
Comment: DOS Setup
run start Wed Sep 27 17:47:09 2000
run finish Wed Sep 27 17:54:19 2000
drive 0x80 (master) no BIOS extensions
3330432 sectors wiped with D1
```

2. partition(src,1,*,Fat 12)

3. partition(src,2,*,Small Fat 16)

4. load_os(DOS)

```
Comment: beta5 D1 (DOS) Layout
Source disk partition table
P 000000063 000024129 0000/001/01 0005/063/63 Boot 01 Fat12
X 000024192 003306240 0006/000/01 0825/063/63       05 extended
S 000000063 000044289 0006/001/01 0016/063/63       04 Fat16
x 000044352 003261888 0017/000/01 0825/063/63       05 extended
S 000000063 003261825 0017/001/01 0825/063/63       06 Fat16
Source disk layout:  00826/064/63 3330432 total sectors on disk
      Start LBA    End LBA    Length    Size: MB   (binary)
  0 B         0         62        63     0.03MB     0.03BMB
  1 P        63      24191     24129    12.35MB    11.78BMB
  2 b     24192      24254        63     0.03MB     0.03BMB
  3 P     24255      68543     44289    22.68MB    21.63BMB
  4 b     68544      68606        63     0.03MB     0.03BMB
  5 P     68607    3330431   3261825  1670.05MB  1592.69BMB
```

5. before=hash(src)

```
A:\DISKHASH.EXE @(#) Version 2.1 Created 09/27/00 at 13:44:51
Comment: hash D1 before running SafeBack
run start Fri Sep 29 11:06:09 2000
run finish Fri Sep 29 12:09:44 2000
drive 0x80 (master) no BIOS extensions
Disk SHA-1 hash 305B31403D8AD36BCB9AF108821818DCFA3F919A
```

6. wipe(dst)

```
A:\DISKWIPE.EXE @(#) Version 2.2 Created 10/02/00 at 09:08:26
Comment: Beta3 setup D11 for DI-07
run start Tue Nov 07 14:09:06 2000
run finish Tue Nov 07 14:23:38 2000
drive 0x81 (slave) no BIOS extensions
12643155 sectors wiped with DB
```

Execute

7. baddisk(dst,write)

```
return code 00010 on command 00003 from disk 00129 (00254 Max head value)
at address 00337/00101/00018
baddisk  compiled on 11/03/00 at 09:12:12
@(#) Version 1.1 Created 11/03/00 at 09:11:04
```

8. copy(src,dst,f,a)

```
        SafeBack 2.0 31Jan00 execution started on Nov  7, 2000 14:43.
14:43:35  Menu selections:
            Function:           Copy
            Remote connection:  Local
            Direct access:      No
            Use XBIOS:          Auto
            Adjust partitions:  Auto
            Backfill on restore: Yes
```

```
            Compress sector data:   Yes
14:43:52  Copy from Local drive 0: to local drive 1:
14:44:05  Copy of Local drive 0: to drive 1: begun on Nov  7, 2000 14:44
14:44:05  Local SafeBack is running on DOS 6.30
14:44:05  Partition table for drive 0:
          Source drive 0:
             Capacity........1628 MB
             Cylinders.......827
             Heads...........64
          Destination drive 1:
             Capacity........6181 MB
             Cylinders.......788
             Heads...........255
14:44:05  Boot sector located at relative sector 63 (Cylinder 0, Head 1, Sector
1)
14:44:09  Boot sector located at relative sector 32193 (Cylinder 2, Head 1,
Sector 1)
14:44:16  Boot sector located at relative sector 80388 (Cylinder 5, Head 1,
Sector 1)
14:53:40  While writing drive 1:, a sector flagged bad error (status 0a)
occurred
          at relative sector 5420285 (Cylinder 337, Head 101, Sector 18)
14:59:29  Partition table for drive 1:
14:59:30  Copy of drive 0: to drive 1: completed on Nov  7, 2000 14:59
          SafeBack execution ended on Nov  7, 2000 15:03.
```

Measure

9. after=hash(src)

```
A:\DISKHASH.EXE @(#) Version 2.2 Created 10/02/00 at 09:08:26
Comment: beta2 hash after DI-07 (D1)
run start Tue Nov 07 15:37:51 2000
run finish Tue Nov 07 16:40:34 2000
drive 0x80 (master) no BIOS extensions
Disk SHA-1 hash 305B31403D8AD36BCB9AF108821818DCFA3F919A
```

10. Examine_message(I/O error)

```
14:53:40  While writing drive 1:, a sector flagged bad error (status 0a)
occurred
```

11. Compare(src,dst)

```
A:\ADJCMP.EXE @(#) Version 2.1 Created 10/10/00 at 15:36:36
Comment: Beta2 DI-07 D1=>D11 with write error at 337/101/18
run start Tue Nov 07 15:07:07 2000
run finish Tue Nov 07 15:36:15 2000
3 partitions, Boot track sectors: compared 189 match 186 differ 3
Data track sectors: compared 3330243 match 3330237 differ 6
Data track sectors filled: zero 9307810 src 3 dst 1 other 4032 remaining 877
```

Output Specifications (expected results)

12. before=after

```
before = 305B31403D8AD36BCB9AF108821818DCFA3F919A
after  = 305B31403D8AD36BCB9AF108821818DCFA3F919A
```

13. I/O error message

```
14:53:40  While writing drive 1:, a sector flagged bad error (status 0a)
occurred
```

14. src and dst compare qualified equal

```
3 partitions, Boot track sectors: compared 189 match 186 differ 3
Data track sectors: compared 3330243 match 3330237 differ 6
```

15. excess dst sectors zero filled

```
Data track sectors filled: zero 9307810 src 3 dst 1 other 4032 remaining 877
```

Test case ID DI-08

Test assertions

1.   If a duplicate copy is created directly from a source disk of the same geometry, then the disks must compare equal.

23.   If the tool encounters any read errors while reading from the source, then the tool must detect and identify the error and notify the user.

27.   If the tool is able to create a destination from an image file that contains read errors, the destination sectors corresponding to the unreadable data must be treated as fill sectors (the tool may allow a specified action or may fill the sectors with zeros).

28.   The source before using the tool must be equal to the source after tool use.

Setup

1. wipe(src)

```
A:\DISKWIPE.EXE @(#) Version 2.1 Created 09/27/00 at 13:44:51
Comment: wipeout slave drive
run start Fri Sep 29 07:53:59 2000
run finish Fri Sep 29 08:18:29 2000
drive 0x81 (slave) use BIOS extensions
30023280 sectors wiped with B1
```

2. partition(src,1,*,NTFS)

3. partition(src,2,*,Fat 32)

4. load_os(Windows 2000)

```
Comment: beta5 B1 W2000 layout
src B0 dst B1
Source disk partition table
P 000000063 004096512 0000/001/01 0254/254/63        07 NTFS
P 004096575 000048195 0255/000/01 0257/254/63        04 Fat16
P 004144770 000096390 0258/000/01 0263/254/63        06 Fat16
X 004241160 025768260 0264/000/01 1023/254/63        0F extended
S 000000063 000016002 0264/001/01 0264/254/63        01 Fat12
x 000016065 000096390 0265/000/01 0270/254/63        05 extended
S 000000063 000096327 0265/001/01 0270/254/63        06 Fat16
x 000112455 002040255 0271/000/01 0397/254/63        05 extended
S 000000063 002040192 0271/001/01 0397/254/63        06 Fat16
x 002152710 002040255 0398/000/01 0524/254/63        05 extended
S 000000063 002040192 0398/001/01 0524/254/63        0B Fat32
x 004192965 021575295 0525/000/01 1023/254/63        05 extended
S 000000063 021575232 0525/001/01 1023/254/63        07 NTFS
Source disk layout:   01023/255/63 16434495 total sectors on disk
        Start LBA    End LBA    Length    Size: MB     (binary)
   0 B         0         62        63      0.03MB      0.03BMB
   1 P        63    4096574   4096512   2097.41MB   2000.25BMB
   2 P   4096575    4144769     48195     24.68MB     23.53BMB
   3 P   4144770    4241159     96390     49.35MB     47.07BMB
   4 b   4241160    4241222        63      0.03MB      0.03BMB
   5 P   4241223    4257224     16002      8.19MB      7.81BMB
   6 b   4257225    4257287        63      0.03MB      0.03BMB
   7 P   4257288    4353614     96327     49.32MB     47.03BMB
   8 b   4353615    4353677        63      0.03MB      0.03BMB
   9 P   4353678    6393869   2040192   1044.58MB    996.19BMB
  10 b   6393870    6393932        63      0.03MB      0.03BMB
  11 P   6393933    8434124   2040192   1044.58MB    996.19BMB
  12 b   8434125    8434187        63      0.03MB      0.03BMB
  13 P   8434188   30009419  21575232  11046.52MB  10534.78BMB
```

5. before=hash(src)

```
A:\DISKHASH.EXE @(#) Version 2.1 Created 09/27/00 at 13:44:51
Comment: Hashing slave (src) before running SafeBack
run start Fri Sep 29 11:16:56 2000
run finish Fri Sep 29 12:44:30 2000
drive 0x81 (slave) use BIOS extensions
Disk SHA-1 hash BB9F63C7247DA70B8C8812AE1EDC1FB58FB9FD98
```

6. wipe(dst)

```
A:\DISKWIPE.EXE @(#) Version 2.2 Created 10/02/00 at 09:08:26
Comment: Beta5 wipe B0
run start Mon Nov 27 09:25:04 2000
run finish Mon Nov 27 09:49:57 2000
drive 0x80 (master) use BIOS extensions
30023280 sectors wiped with B0
```

Execute

7. baddisk(src,read)

```
badx13    compiled on 11/24/00 at 17:14:42
@(#) Version 1.1 Created 11/24/00 at 17:14:28
Return error code 10 for X13 command 42 from drive 81 at LBA sector 1,000,000
```

8. copy(src,dst)

```
          SafeBack 2.0 31Jan00 execution started on Nov 27, 2000 11:40.
11:40:51  Menu selections:
                Function:              Copy
                Remote connection:     Local
                Direct access:         No
                Use XBIOS:             Auto
                Adjust partitions:     Auto
                Backfill on restore:   Yes
                Compress sector data:  Yes
11:41:06  Copy from Local drive 1: to local drive 0:
11:41:14  Copy of Local drive 1: to drive 0: begun on Nov 27, 2000 11:41
11:41:14  Local SafeBack is running on DOS 6.30
11:41:14  Partition table for drive 1:
          Source drive 1:
              Capacity........14660 MB
              Cylinders.......1868
              Heads...........255
          Destination drive 0:
              Capacity........14660 MB
              Cylinders.......1868
              Heads...........255
11:42:25  While reading drive 1: a sector flagged bad error (status 0a)
occurred:
          at relative sector 1000000 (Cylinder 62, Head 63, Sector 2)
12:16:48  Partition table for drive 0:
12:16:49  Copy of drive 1: to drive 0: completed on Nov 27, 2000 12:16
          SafeBack execution ended on Nov 27, 2000 12:26.
```

Measure

9. after=hash(src)

```
A:\DISKHASH.EXE @(#) Version 2.2 Created 10/02/00 at 09:08:26
Comment: Beta5 DI-08 hash after running SafeBack
run start Mon Nov 27 14:29:26 2000
run finish Mon Nov 27 15:56:51 2000
drive 0x81 (slave) use BIOS extensions
Disk SHA-1 hash BB9F63C7247DA70B8C8812AE1EDC1FB58FB9FD98
```

10. Examine_message(I/O error)
```
11:42:25  While reading drive 1: a sector flagged bad error (status 0a)
occurred:
```
11. Compare(src,dst)
```
Comment: beta5 DI-08
run start Mon Nov 27 13:51:06 2000
run finish Mon Nov 27 14:26:27 2000
sectors compared 30023280 match 30023279 differ 1 dropped 0
filled: zero 0 src 0 dst 0 other 0 remainder 0
```
   Output Specifications (expected results)
12. before=after
```
before = BB9F63C7247DA70B8C8812AE1EDC1FB58FB9FD98
after  = BB9F63C7247DA70B8C8812AE1EDC1FB58FB9FD98
```
13. I/O error message
```
11:42:25  While reading drive 1: a sector flagged bad error (status 0a)
occurred:
```
14. src and dst compare qualified equal
```
sectors compared 30023280 match 30023279 differ 1 dropped 0
```

Note: Two disks *compare qualified equal* if there exists at least one *non-comparable region* (defined below) and if ignoring sectors in all non-comparable regions, the disks compare equal or adjusted equal as appropriate.

A *non-comparable region* is a contiguous set of corresponding sectors that contains at least one *non-comparable sector pair.*

A *non-comparable sector pair* is a pair of corresponding sectors if at least one of the following is true:
1. The source sector cannot be read.
2. The destination sector cannot be written.
3. At least one byte from the source sector is contained in a sector that cannot be read of an image file created from the source and used to create the destination.

Test case ID DI-09

Test assertions
1.   If a duplicate copy is created directly from a source disk of the same geometry, then the disks must compare equal.
26.   If the tool encounters any write errors while writing to the destination, then the tool must detect and identify the error and notify the user.
28.   The source before using the tool must be equal to the source after tool use.
   Setup
1. wipe(src)
```
A:\DISKWIPE.EXE @(#) Version 2.1 Created 09/27/00 at 13:44:51
Comment: wipeout slave drive
run start Fri Sep 29 07:53:59 2000
run finish Fri Sep 29 08:18:29 2000
drive 0x81 (slave) use BIOS extensions
30023280 sectors wiped with B1
```
2. partition(src,1,*,NTFS)
3. partition(src,2,*,Fat 32)

4. load_os(Windows 2000)
Comment: beta5 B1 W2000 layout
src B0 dst B1
Source disk partition table
P 000000063 004096512 0000/001/01 0254/254/63   07 NTFS
P 004096575 000048195 0255/000/01 0257/254/63   04 Fat16
P 004144770 000096390 0258/000/01 0263/254/63   06 Fat16
X 004241160 025768260 0264/000/01 1023/254/63   0F extended
S 000000063 000016002 0264/001/01 0264/254/63   01 Fat12
x 000016065 000096390 0265/000/01 0270/254/63   05 extended
S 000000063 000096327 0265/001/01 0270/254/63   06 Fat16
x 000112455 002040255 0271/000/01 0397/254/63   05 extended
S 000000063 002040192 0271/001/01 0397/254/63   06 Fat16
x 002152710 002040255 0398/000/01 0524/254/63   05 extended
S 000000063 002040192 0398/001/01 0524/254/63   0B Fat32
x 004192965 021575295 0525/000/01 1023/254/63   05 extended
S 000000063 021575232 0525/001/01 1023/254/63   07 NTFS
Source disk layout: 01023/255/63 16434495 total sectors on disk
        Start LBA   End LBA   Length   Size: MB   (binary)
  0 B   0   62   63   0.03MB   0.03BMB
  1 P   63   4096574   4096512 2097.41MB 2000.25BMB
  2 P   4096575   4144769   48195   24.68MB   23.53BMB
  3 P   4144770   4241159   96390   49.35MB   47.07BMB
  4 b   4241160   4241222   63   0.03MB   0.03BMB
  5 P   4241223   4257224   16002   8.19MB   7.81BMB
  6 b   4257225   4257287   63   0.03MB   0.03BMB
  7 P   4257288   4353614   96327   49.32MB   47.03BMB
  8 b   4353615   4353677   63   0.03MB   0.03BMB
  9 P   4353678   6393869   2040192 1044.58MB   996.19BMB
 10 b   6393870   6393932   63   0.03MB   0.03BMB
 11 P   6393933   8434124   2040192 1044.58MB   996.19BMB
 12 b   8434125   8434187   63   0.03MB   0.03BMB
 13 P   8434188   30009419 21575232 11046.52MB 10534.78BMB
5. before=hash(src)
A:\DISKHASH.EXE @(#) Version 2.1 Created 09/27/00 at 13:44:51
Comment: Hashing slave (src) before running SafeBack
run start Fri Sep 29 11:16:56 2000
run finish Fri Sep 29 12:44:30 2000
drive 0x81 (slave) use BIOS extensions
Disk SHA-1 hash BB9F63C7247DA70B8C8812AE1EDC1FB58FB9FD98
6. wipe(dst)
A:\DISKWIPE.EXE @(#) Version 2.2 Created 10/02/00 at 09:08:26
Comment: Beta5 DI-09
run start Mon Nov 27 16:17:11 2000
run finish Mon Nov 27 16:41:36 2000
drive 0x80 (master) use BIOS extensions
30023280 sectors wiped with B0
   Execute
7. baddisk(dst,write)
badx13   compiled on 11/24/00 at 17:14:42
@(#) Version 1.1 Created 11/24/00 at 17:14:28
Return error code 10 for X13 command 43 from drive 80 at LBA sector 2,000,000

8. copy(src,dst)
        SafeBack 2.0 31Jan00 execution started on Nov 27, 2000 16:56.

```
16:57:04  Menu selections:
              Function:             Copy
              Remote connection:    Local
              Direct access:        No
              Use XBIOS:            Auto
              Adjust partitions:    Auto
              Backfill on restore:  Yes
              Compress sector data: Yes
16:57:17  Menu selections:
              Function:             Copy
              Remote connection:    Local
              Direct access:        No
              Use XBIOS:            Auto
              Adjust partitions:    Auto
              Backfill on restore:  Yes
              Compress sector data: Yes
16:57:23  Copy from Local drive 1: to local drive 0:
16:57:31  Copy of Local drive 1: to drive 0: begun on Nov 27, 2000 16:57
16:57:31  Local SafeBack is running on DOS 6.30
16:57:31  Partition table for drive 1:
          Source drive 1:
              Capacity........14660 MB
              Cylinders.......1868
              Heads...........255
          Destination drive 0:
              Capacity........14660 MB
              Cylinders.......1868
              Heads...........255
16:59:52  While writing drive 0:, a sector flagged bad error (status 0a)
occurred
              at relative sector 2000000 (Cylinder 124, Head 126, Sector 3)
17:32:51  Partition table for drive 0:
17:32:52  Copy of drive 1: to drive 0: completed on Nov 27, 2000 17:32
              SafeBack execution ended on Nov 27, 2000 17:33.
```

Measure

9. after=hash(src)

```
A:\DISKHASH.EXE @(#) Version 2.2 Created 10/02/00 at 09:08:26
Comment: beta5 hash after DI-09
run start Tue Nov 28 09:19:58 2000
run finish Tue Nov 28 10:47:19 2000
drive 0x81 (slave) use BIOS extensions
Disk SHA-1 hash BB9F63C7247DA70B8C8812AE1EDC1FB58FB9FD98
```

10. Examine_message(I/O error)

```
16:59:52  While writing drive 0:, a sector flagged bad error (status 0a)
occurred
```

11. Compare(src,dst)

```
Comment: Beta5 DI-09 write error at LBA 2000000
run start Mon Nov 27 17:35:17 2000
run finish Mon Nov 27 18:10:52 2000
sectors compared 30023280 match 30023247 differ 33 dropped 0
filled: zero 0 src 0 dst 0 other 0 remainder 0
```

Output Specifications (expected results)

12. before=after

```
before = BB9F63C7247DA70B8C8812AE1EDC1FB58FB9FD98
after  = BB9F63C7247DA70B8C8812AE1EDC1FB58FB9FD98
```

13. I/O error message

```
16:59:52  While writing drive 0:, a sector flagged bad error (status 0a)
occurred
```
14. src and dst compare qualified equal
```
sectors compared 30023280 match 30023247 differ 33 dropped 0
```

Test case ID DI-10

Test assertions

1.   *If a duplicate copy is created directly from a source disk of the same geometry, then the disks must compare equal.*

28.   *The source before using the tool must be equal to the source after tool use.*

29.   *The results of any remote tool use must be equal to the results of local identical tool use.*

  Setup

1. wipe(src)
```
A:\DISKWIPE.EXE @(#) Version 2.1 Created 09/27/00 at 13:44:51
Comment: Windows 95 setup
run start Wed Sep 27 17:52:35 2000
run finish Wed Sep 27 17:59:47 2000
drive 0x80 (master) no BIOS extensions
3330432 sectors wiped with F1
```
2. partition(src,1,*,Big Fat 16)

3. load_os(Windows 95)
```
Comment: beta5 F1 W95 layout
Source disk partition table
P 000000063 003072321 0000/001/01 0761/063/63 Boot 06 Fat16
X 003072384 000258048 0762/000/01 0825/063/63      05 extended
S 000000063 000104769 0762/001/01 0787/063/63      06 Fat16
x 000104832 000153216 0788/000/01 0825/063/63      05 extended
S 000000063 000153153 0788/001/01 0825/063/63      06 Fat16
Source disk layout:  00826/064/63 3330432 total sectors on disk
      Start LBA    End LBA    Length    Size: MB    (binary)
  0 B         0         62        63      0.03MB     0.03BMB
  1 P        63    3072383   3072321   1573.03MB  1500.16BMB
  2 b   3072384    3072446        63      0.03MB     0.03BMB
  3 P   3072447    3177215    104769     53.64MB    51.16BMB
  4 b   3177216    3177278        63      0.03MB     0.03BMB
  5 P   3177279    3330431    153153     78.41MB    74.78BMB
```
4. before=hash(src)
```
A:\DISKHASH.EXE @(#) Version 2.2 Created 10/02/00 at 09:08:26
Comment: rehash F1 (Win 95)
run start Fri Nov 03 14:08:19 2000
run finish Fri Nov 03 14:28:46 2000
drive 0x80 (master) no BIOS extensions
Disk SHA-1 hash 5FBEEB219E7282ED621645A67252A70F4D8BBF21
```
5. wipe(dst)
```
A:\DISKWIPE.EXE @(#) Version 2.2 Created 10/02/00 at 09:08:26
Comment: DI-10 Wipe D2 on Beta5
run start Sat Nov 18 13:03:24 2000
run finish Sat Nov 18 13:11:37 2000
drive 0x80 (master) no BIOS extensions
3330432 sectors wiped with D2
```
  Execute

6. establish_link()

7. copy(src,dst)
```
        SafeBack 2.0 31Jan00 execution started on Nov 18, 2000 13:23.
```

34

```
13:23:46  Menu selections:
              Function:            Copy
              Remote connection:   LPT1:
              Direct access:       No
              Use XBIOS:           Auto
              Adjust partitions:   Auto
              Backfill on restore: Yes
              Compress sector data: Yes
13:24:09  Copy from Remote drive 0: to local drive 0:
13:24:19  Copy of Remote drive 0: to drive 0: begun on Nov 18, 2000 13:24
13:24:19  Local SafeBack is running on DOS 6.30
13:24:19  Remote SafeBack server is running on DOS 6.30
13:24:19  Partition table for drive 0:
          Source drive 0:
             Capacity........1628 MB
             Cylinders.......827
             Heads...........64
          Destination drive 0:
             Capacity........1628 MB
             Cylinders.......827
             Heads...........64
22:03:36  Partition table for drive 0:
22:03:36  Copy of drive 0: to drive 0: completed on Nov 18, 2000 22:03
          SafeBack execution ended on Nov 19, 2000 10:42.
```

Measure

8. after=hash(src)

```
A:\DISKHASH.EXE @(#) Version 2.2 Created 10/02/00 at 09:08:26
Comment: beta5 DI-10 hash F1 after running SafeBack
run start Sun Nov 19 11:50:17 2000
run finish Sun Nov 19 12:10:50 2000
drive 0x80 (master) no BIOS extensions
Disk SHA-1 hash 5FBEEB219E7282ED621645A67252A70F4D8BBF21
```

9. Compare(src,dst)

```
Comment: beta2 DI-10 F1==>D2
run start Sun Nov 19 10:45:57 2000
run finish Sun Nov 19 10:57:23 2000
sectors compared 3330432 match 3330432 differ 0 dropped 0
filled: zero 0 src 0 dst 0 other 0 remainder 0
```

Output Specifications (expected results)

10. before=after

```
before = 5FBEEB219E7282ED621645A67252A70F4D8BBF21
after  = 5FBEEB219E7282ED621645A67252A70F4D8BBF21
```

11. src and dst compare equal

```
sectors compared 3330432 match 3330432 differ 0 dropped 0
```

Test case ID DI-11

Test assertions

3.   If a duplicate copy is created directly from a source disk of a smaller geometry and cylinder adjustment is not enabled, then the disks must compare equal.

4.   If a duplicate copy is created directly from a source disk of smaller geometry, then the contents of the destination disk sectors not corresponding to source disk sectors must be as specified by the tool (if the tool allows such a specification). Otherwise each bit of such sectors must be set to zero.

23. *If the tool encounters any read errors while reading from the source, then the tool must detect and identify the error and notify the user.*

27. *If the tool is able to create a destination from an image file that contains read errors, the destination sectors corresponding to the unreadable data must be treated as fill sectors (the tool may allow a specified action or may fill the sectors with zeros).*

28. *The source before using the tool must be equal to the source after tool use.*

29. *The results of any remote tool use must be equal to the results of local identical tool use.*

Setup

1. wipe(src)

```
A:\DISKWIPE.EXE @(#) Version 2.1 Created 09/27/00 at 13:44:51
Comment: Windows 98 setup
run start Wed Sep 27 17:40:45 2000
run finish Wed Sep 27 17:48:08 2000
drive 0x80 (master) no BIOS extensions
3330432 sectors wiped with F2
```

2. partition(src,1,*,Fat 32)

3. load_os(Windows 98)

```
Comment: beta5 F2 (W98) layout
Source disk partition table
P 000000063 001640961 0000/001/01 0406/063/63 Boot 0B Fat32
X 001641024 001689408 0407/000/01 0825/063/63      05 extended
S 000000063 001640961 0407/001/01 0813/063/63      0B Fat32
x 001641024 000048384 0814/000/01 0825/063/63      05 extended
S 000000063 000048321 0814/001/01 0825/063/63      04 Fat16
Source disk layout:  00826/064/63 3330432 total sectors on disk
      Start LBA    End LBA    Length     Size: MB    (binary)
 0 B          0         62        63     0.03MB     0.03BMB
 1 P         63    1641023   1640961   840.17MB   801.25BMB
 2 b    1641024    1641086        63     0.03MB     0.03BMB
 3 P    1641087    3282047   1640961   840.17MB   801.25BMB
 4 b    3282048    3282110        63     0.03MB     0.03BMB
 5 P    3282111    3330431     48321    24.74MB    23.59BMB
```

4. before=hash(src)

```
A:\DISKHASH.EXE @(#) Version 2.1 Created 09/27/00 at 13:44:51
Comment: reference hash for F2
run start Fri Sep 29 11:46:04 2000
run finish Fri Sep 29 12:49:43 2000
drive 0x80 (master) no BIOS extensions
Disk SHA-1 hash 96EDE9BC7D9A33A61A5537C5CB7DF45CAD6ED488
```

5. wipe(dst)

```
A:\DISKWIPE.EXE @(#) Version 2.2 Created 10/02/00 at 09:08:26
Comment: beta5 wipe D11 for DI-11
run start Mon Dec 18 18:19:01 2000
run finish Mon Dec 18 18:31:02 2000
drive 0x80 (master) no BIOS extensions
12643155 sectors wiped with DB
```

Execute

6. establish_link()

7. baddisk(src,read)

```
return code 00010 on command 00002 from disk 00128 (00063 Max head value)
at address 00300/00000/00001
baddisk  compiled on 11/03/00 at 09:12:12
@(#) Version 1.1 Created 11/03/00 at 09:11:04
return code 00010 on command 00010 from disk 00128 (00063 Max head value)
```

36

```
at address 00300/00000/00001
baddisk  compiled on 11/03/00 at 09:12:12
@(#) Version 1.1 Created 11/03/00 at 09:11:04
```

8. copy(src,dst,n,n)

```
          SafeBack 2.0 31Jan00 execution started on Dec 18, 2000 17:40.
17:40:40  Menu selections:
               Function:              Copy
               Remote connection:     LPT1:
               Direct access:         No
               Use XBIOS:             Auto
               Adjust partitions:     No
               Backfill on restore:   No
               Compress sector data:  Yes
17:41:05  Copy from Remote drive 0: to local drive 0:
17:41:21  Copy of Remote drive 0: to drive 0: begun on Dec 18, 2000 17:41
17:41:21  Local SafeBack is running on DOS 6.30
17:41:21  Remote SafeBack server is running on DOS 6.30
17:41:21  Partition table for drive 0:
          Source drive 0:
               Capacity........1628 MB
               Cylinders.......827
               Heads...........64
          Destination drive 0:
               Capacity........6181 MB
               Cylinders.......788
               Heads...........255
20:44:52  While reading drive 0: a sector flagged bad error (status 0a)
occurred:
          at relative sector 1209600 (Cylinder 300, Head 0, Sector 1)
02:28:13  Copy of drive 0: to drive 0: completed on Dec 19, 2000 02:28
          SafeBack execution ended on Dec 19, 2000 08:07.
```

Measure

9. after=hash(src)

```
A:\DISKHASH.EXE %Z% Version %I% Created %G% at %U%
Comment: beta5 DI-11
run start Tue Dec 19 10:02:54 2000
run finish Tue Dec 19 10:23:21 2000
drive 0x80 (master) no BIOS extensions
Disk SHA-1 hash 96EDE9BC7D9A33A61A5537C5CB7DF45CAD6ED488
```

10. Examine_message(I/O error)

```
20:44:52  While reading drive 0: a sector flagged bad error (status 0a)
occurred:
```

11. Compare(src,dst)

```
Comment: DI-11 beta2:F2==>beta3:D11 (compare on beta2)
run start Tue Dec 19 09:11:18 2000
run finish Tue Dec 19 09:41:30 2000
sectors compared 3330432 match 3330431 differ 1 dropped 0
filled: zero 9308691 src 0  dst 0  other 4032 remainder 0
```

Output Specifications (expected results)

12. before=after

```
before = 96EDE9BC7D9A33A61A5537C5CB7DF45CAD6ED488
after  = 96EDE9BC7D9A33A61A5537C5CB7DF45CAD6ED488
```

13. I/O error message

```
20:44:52  While reading drive 0: a sector flagged bad error (status 0a)
occurred:
```

14. src and dst compare qualified equal
```
sectors compared 3330432 match 3330431 differ 1 dropped 0
```

Test case ID DI-12

Test assertions

7. *If a duplicate destination disk is created from an image file of a source disk with the same geometry, then the disks must compare equal.*

28. *The source before using the tool must be equal to the source after tool use.*

Setup

1. wipe(src)
```
A:\DISKWIPE.EXE @(#) Version 2.1 Created 09/27/00 at 13:44:51
Comment: Linux setup
run start Thu Sep 28 14:49:16 2000
run finish Thu Sep 28 14:56:29 2000
drive 0x80 (master) no BIOS extensions
3330432 sectors wiped with D4
```

2. partition(src,1,*,Linux)
3. partition(src,2,*,Linux Swap)
4. load_os(Linux)
```
Comment: D4 (linux) layout
Source disk partition table
P 000000063 002048193 0000/001/01 0507/063/63 Boot 83 Linux
X 002048256 001286208 0508/000/01 0826/063/63      05 extended
S 000000063 000205569 0508/001/01 0558/063/63      82 Linux swap
x 000205632 001080576 0559/000/01 0826/063/63      05 extended
S 000000063 001080513 0559/001/01 0826/063/63      83 Linux
Source disk layout:  00826/064/63 3330432 total sectors on disk
      Start LBA    End LBA    Length    Size: MB   (binary)
  0 B         0         62        63     0.03MB    0.03BMB
  1 P        63    2048255   2048193  1048.67MB  1000.09BMB
  2 b   2048256    2048318        63     0.03MB    0.03BMB
  3 P   2048319    2253887    205569   105.25MB   100.38BMB
  4 b   2253888    2253950        63     0.03MB    0.03BMB
  5 P   2253951    3334463   1080513   553.22MB   527.59BMB
```

5. before=hash(src)
```
A:\DISKHASH.EXE @(#) Version 2.2 Created 10/02/00 at 09:08:26
Comment: beta5, hash d4 for test DI-12
run start Thu Oct 12 08:39:28 2000
run finish Thu Oct 12 08:59:54 2000
drive 0x80 (master) no BIOS extensions
Disk SHA-1 hash D25C035B74F3EECFCBA4A1968AA6D48096D92EE2
```

6. wipe(img)
7. partition(img,1,MAX,Big Fat 16)
8. wipe(dst)
```
A:\DISKWIPE.EXE @(#) Version 2.2 Created 10/02/00 at 09:08:26
Comment: beta5, wipe D2 for DI-12
run start Thu Oct 12 08:28:01 2000
run finish Thu Oct 12 08:35:37 2000
drive 0x80 (master) no BIOS extensions
3330432 sectors wiped with D2
```

Execute

9. image(src,img.1)
```
        SafeBack 2.0 31Jan00 execution started on Oct 12, 2000 09:08.
```

```
09:08:38   Menu selections:
               Function:              Backup
               Remote connection:     Local
               Direct access:         No
               Use XBIOS:             Auto
               Adjust partitions:     Auto
               Backfill on restore:   Yes
               Compress sector data:  Yes
09:09:48   Backup file D:\D4T12.001 created.
           Backup file comment record:
               Disk image test DI-12 on beta4, D4->D3->D2
09:10:36   Backing up drive 0:
               to D:\D4T12.001 on Oct 12, 2000 09:10
09:10:38   Local SafeBack is running on DOS 6.30
           Source drive 0:
               Capacity........1628 MB
               Cylinders.......827
               Heads...........64
09:10:38   Partition table for drive 0:
09:22:20   Backup file CRC: 9d30bdc0.
09:22:20   Backup of drive 0: completed on Oct 12, 2000 09:22.
           SafeBack execution ended on Oct 12, 2000 09:25.
```

10. load(img.1,dst)

```
           SafeBack 2.0 31Jan00 execution started on Oct 12, 2000 09:31.
09:31:43   Menu selections:
               Function:              Restore
               Remote connection:     Local
               Direct access:         No
               Use XBIOS:             Auto
               Adjust partitions:     Auto
               Backfill on restore:   Yes
               Compress sector data:  Yes
09:32:07   Backup file created on Oct 12, 2000 09:10
               by Gary Fisher Natl Institute of Standards & Technology Software
Diagnostics & Con
           Backup file comment record:
               Disk image test DI-12 on beta4, D4->D3->D2
09:32:17   Backup file D:\D4T12.001 opened for access.
09:32:42   Restore of drive 0: from D:\D4T12.001
               to drive 0: started on Oct 12, 2000 09:32
09:32:42   Local SafeBack is running on DOS 6.30
           Source drive 0:
               Capacity........1628 MB
               Cylinders.......827
               Heads...........64
           Destination drive 0:
               Capacity........1628 MB
               Cylinders.......827
               Heads...........64
09:46:36   The whole-file CRC verifies:  9d30bdc0
09:46:47   Partition table for drive 0:
09:46:49   Restore of drive 0: to drive 0: completed on Oct 12, 2000 09:46
09:47:01   Menu selections:
               Function:              Restore
               Remote connection:     Local
               Direct access:         No
               Use XBIOS:             Auto
               Adjust partitions:     Auto
```

```
            Backfill on restore:      Yes
            Compress sector data:     Yes
        SafeBack execution ended on Oct 12, 2000 09:47.
```
Measure

11. after=hash(src)
```
A:\DISKHASH.EXE @(#) Version 2.2 Created 10/02/00 at 09:08:26
Comment: beta5, test di-12, hash after SafeBack
run start Thu Oct 12 09:28:19 2000
run finish Thu Oct 12 09:48:36 2000
drive 0x80 (master) no BIOS extensions
Disk SHA-1 hash D25C035B74F3EECFCBA4A1968AA6D48096D92EE2
```

12. Compare(src,dst)
```
Comment: beta4 D2->D3->D4 Test DI-12
run start Thu Oct 12 12:56:26 2000
run finish Thu Oct 12 13:08:03 2000
sectors compared 3330432 match 3330432 differ 0 dropped 0
filled: zero 0 src 0 dst 0 other 0 remainder 0
```
Output Specifications (expected results)

13. before=after
```
before = D25C035B74F3EECFCBA4A1968AA6D48096D92EE2
after  = D25C035B74F3EECFCBA4A1968AA6D48096D92EE2
```
14. src and dst compare equal
```
sectors compared 3330432 match 3330432 differ 0 dropped 0
```

Test case ID DI-13

Test assertions

11.   If a duplicate destination disk is created from an image file of a source disk with a larger geometry, then the tool must notify the user.

12.   If a duplicate destination disk is created from an image file of a source disk with a larger geometry, then every sector of the destination disk must compare equal to the corresponding sector on the source disk.

28.   The source before using the tool must be equal to the source after tool use.

Setup

1. wipe(src)
```
A:\DISKWIPE.EXE @(#) Version 2.1 Created 09/27/00 at 13:44:51
Comment: DOS Setup
run start Wed Sep 27 17:47:09 2000
run finish Wed Sep 27 17:54:19 2000
drive 0x80 (master) no BIOS extensions
3330432 sectors wiped with D1
```
2. partition(src,1,*,Fat 12)
3. partition(src,2,*,Small Fat 16)
4. load_os(DOS)
```
Comment: beta5 D1 (DOS) Layout
Source disk partition table
P 000000063 000024129 0000/001/01 0005/063/63 Boot 01 Fat12
X 000024192 003306240 0006/000/01 0825/063/63      05 extended
S 000000063 000044289 0006/001/01 0016/063/63      04 Fat16
x 000044352 003261888 0017/000/01 0825/063/63      05 extended
S 000000063 003261825 0017/001/01 0825/063/63      06 Fat16
Source disk layout:  00826/064/63 3330432 total sectors on disk
      Start LBA    End LBA    Length    Size: MB   (binary)
  0 B         0         62        63    0.03MB     0.03BMB
```

40

```
1 P         63     24191     24129     12.35MB     11.78BMB
2 b      24192     24254        63      0.03MB      0.03BMB
3 P      24255     68543     44289     22.68MB     21.63BMB
4 b      68544     68606        63      0.03MB      0.03BMB
5 P      68607   3330431   3261825   1670.05MB   1592.69BMB
```

5. before=hash(src)

```
A:\DISKHASH.EXE @(#) Version 2.1 Created 09/27/00 at 13:44:51
Comment: hash D1 before running SafeBack
run start Fri Sep 29 11:06:09 2000
run finish Fri Sep 29 12:09:44 2000
drive 0x80 (master) no BIOS extensions
Disk SHA-1 hash 305B31403D8AD36BCB9AF108821818DCFA3F919A
```

6. wipe(img)

7. partition(img,1,MAX,Big Fat 16)

8. wipe(dst)

```
A:\DISKWIPE.EXE @(#) Version 2.2 Created 10/02/00 at 09:08:26
Comment: beta5 DI-13
run start Sun Dec 03 16:14:52 2000
run finish Sun Dec 03 16:29:32 2000
drive 0x80 (master) no BIOS extensions
2495808 sectors wiped with D5
```

   Execute

9. image(src,img.1)

```
            SafeBack 2.0 31Jan00 execution started on Dec  3, 2000 16:10.
16:10:27  Menu selections:
              Function:             Backup
              Remote connection:    Local
              Direct access:        No
              Use XBIOS:            Auto
              Adjust partitions:    Auto
              Backfill on restore:  Yes
              Compress sector data: Yes
16:11:19  Backup file H:\D1T13.001 created.
          Backup file comment record:
              Test DI-13 D1->D3 H:\D1T13 ->D5 (beta2)
16:12:16  Backing up drive 0:
          to H:\D1T13.001 on Dec  3, 2000 16:12
16:12:17  Local SafeBack is running on DOS 6.30
          Source drive 0:
              Capacity........1628 MB
              Cylinders.......827
              Heads...........64
16:12:17  Partition table for drive 0:
16:24:14  Backup file CRC: 5c9e36e8.
16:24:14  Backup of drive 0: completed on Dec  3, 2000 16:24.
          SafeBack execution ended on Dec  3, 2000 16:24.
```

10. load(img.1,dst)

```
            SafeBack 2.0 31Jan00 execution started on Dec  3, 2000 16:39.
16:39:26  Menu selections:
              Function:             Restore
              Remote connection:    Local
              Direct access:        No
              Use XBIOS:            Auto
              Adjust partitions:    Auto
              Backfill on restore:  Yes
              Compress sector data: Yes
```

```
16:39:40  Backup file created on Dec  3, 2000 16:12
          by Gary Fisher Natl Institute of Standards & Technology Software
Diagnostics & Con
          Backup file comment record:
            Test DI-13 D1->D3 H:\D1T13 ->D5 (beta2)
16:39:43  Backup file E:\D1T13.001 opened for access.
16:39:58  The destination drive capacity is smaller than that of the
          original source drive.
16:40:10  Restore of drive 0: from E:\D1T13.001
          to drive 0: started on Dec  3, 2000 16:40
16:40:10  Local SafeBack is running on DOS 6.30
          Source drive 0:
            Capacity........1628 MB
            Cylinders.......827
            Heads...........64
          Destination drive 0:
            Capacity........1221 MB
            Cylinders.......620
            Heads...........64
17:03:25  Partition table for drive 0:
17:03:26  Restore of drive 0: to drive 0: completed on Dec  3, 2000 17:03
17:05:39  Menu selections:
            Function:           Restore
            Remote connection:  Local
            Direct access:      No
            Use XBIOS:          Auto
            Adjust partitions:  Auto
            Backfill on restore: Yes
            Compress sector data: Yes
          SafeBack execution ended on Dec  3, 2000 17:05.
```

Measure

11. after=hash(src)
```
A:\DISKHASH.EXE %Z% Version %I% Created %G% at %U%
Comment: beta5 hash D1 after DI-13
run start Sun Dec 03 17:24:56 2000
run finish Sun Dec 03 17:45:17 2000
drive 0x80 (master) no BIOS extensions
Disk SHA-1 hash 305B31403D8AD36BCB9AF108821818DCFA3F919A
```

12. Examine_message(Destination too small)
```
16:39:58  The destination drive capacity is smaller than that of the
          original source drive.
```

13. Compare(src,dst)
```
Comment: beta2 DI-13 D1 ->D5
run start Sun Dec 03 17:07:54 2000
run finish Sun Dec 03 17:17:44 2000
sectors compared 2495808 match 2495808 differ 0 dropped 834624
filled: zero 0 src 0 dst 0 other 0 remainder 0
```

Output Specifications (expected results)

14. before=after
```
before = 305B31403D8AD36BCB9AF108821818DCFA3F919A
after  = 305B31403D8AD36BCB9AF108821818DCFA3F919A
```

15. Destination too small message
```
16:39:58  The destination drive capacity is smaller than that of the
          original source drive.
```

16. src and dst compare equal
```
sectors compared 2495808 match 2495808 differ 0 dropped 834624
```

Test case ID DI-14

Test assertions

8.   *If a duplicate destination disk is created from an image file of a source disk with a smaller geometry and cylinder adjustment is enabled, then the disks must compare adjusted equal.*

10.   *If a duplicate destination disk is created from an image file of a source disk with a smaller geometry, then the contents of the destination disk sectors not corresponding to source disk sectors must be as specified by the tool (if the tool allows such a specification). Otherwise each bit of such sectors must be set to zero.*

28.   *The source before using the tool must be equal to the source after tool use.*

Setup

1. wipe(src)

```
A:\DISKWIPE.EXE @(#) Version 2.1 Created 09/27/00 at 13:44:51
Comment: Windows 95 setup
run start Wed Sep 27 17:52:35 2000
run finish Wed Sep 27 17:59:47 2000
drive 0x80 (master) no BIOS extensions
3330432 sectors wiped with F1
```

2. partition(src,1,*,Big Fat 16)

3. load_os(Windows 95)

```
Comment: beta5 F1 W95 layout
Source disk partition table
P 000000063 003072321 0000/001/01 0761/063/63 Boot 06 Fat16
X 003072384 000258048 0762/000/01 0825/063/63      05 extended
S 000000063 000104769 0762/001/01 0787/063/63      06 Fat16
x 000104832 000153216 0788/000/01 0825/063/63      05 extended
S 000000063 000153153 0788/001/01 0825/063/63      06 Fat16
Source disk layout:  00826/064/63 3330432 total sectors on disk
      Start LBA    End LBA    Length    Size: MB   (binary)
  0 B         0         62         63    0.03MB    0.03BMB
  1 P        63   3072383    3072321 1573.03MB 1500.16BMB
  2 b   3072384   3072446         63    0.03MB    0.03BMB
  3 P   3072447   3177215     104769   53.64MB   51.16BMB
  4 b   3177216   3177278         63    0.03MB    0.03BMB
  5 P   3177279   3330431     153153   78.41MB   74.78BMB
```

4. before=hash(src)

```
A:\DISKHASH.EXE @(#) Version 2.2 Created 10/02/00 at 09:08:26
Comment: rehash F1 (Win 95)
run start Fri Nov 03 14:08:19 2000
run finish Fri Nov 03 14:28:46 2000
drive 0x80 (master) no BIOS extensions
Disk SHA-1 hash 5FBEEB219E7282ED621645A67252A70F4D8BBF21
```

5. wipe(img)

6. partition(img,1,MAX,Big Fat 16)

7. wipe(dst)

```
A:\DISKWIPE.EXE @(#) Version 2.2 Created 10/02/00 at 09:08:26
Comment: beta4 wipe D11 for DI-14
run start Tue Nov 28 11:43:12 2000
run finish Tue Nov 28 11:54:07 2000
drive 0x80 (master) no BIOS extensions
12643155 sectors wiped with DB
```

Execute

8. image(src,img.1,n,a)

```
        SafeBack 2.0 31Jan00 execution started on Nov 28, 2000 12:18.
```

```
12:18:27  Menu selections:
                Function:              Backup
                Remote connection:     Local
                Direct access:         No
                Use XBIOS:             Auto
                Adjust partitions:     Auto
                Backfill on restore:   No
                Compress sector data:  Yes
12:19:11  Backup file D:\F1T14.001 created.
          Backup file comment record:
                beta2 DI-14 F1->D3(D:\F1T14)->D11
12:19:54  Backing up drive 0:
          to D:\F1T14.001 on Nov 28, 2000 12:19
12:19:55  Local SafeBack is running on DOS 6.30
          Source drive 0:
                Capacity........1628 MB
                Cylinders.......827
                Heads...........64
12:19:55  Partition table for drive 0:
12:31:55  Backup file CRC: 22c1b141.
12:31:55  Backup of drive 0: completed on Nov 28, 2000 12:31.
          SafeBack execution ended on Nov 28, 2000 12:33.
```

9. load(img.1,dst)

```
          SafeBack 2.0 31Jan00 execution started on Nov 28, 2000 12:36.
12:36:35  Menu selections:
                Function:              Restore
                Remote connection:     Local
                Direct access:         No
                Use XBIOS:             Auto
                Adjust partitions:     Auto
                Backfill on restore:   No
                Compress sector data:  Yes
12:36:46  Backup file created on Nov 28, 2000 12:19
          by Gary Fisher Natl Institute of Standards & Technology Software
Diagnostics & Con
          Backup file comment record:
                beta2 DI-14 F1->D3(D:\F1T14)->D11
12:36:49  Backup file C:\F1T14.001 opened for access.
12:37:24  Restore of drive 0: from C:\F1T14.001
          to drive 0: started on Nov 28, 2000 12:37
12:37:24  Local SafeBack is running on DOS 6.30
          Source drive 0:
                Capacity........1628 MB
                Cylinders.......827
                Heads...........64
          Destination drive 0:
                Capacity........6181 MB
                Cylinders.......788
                Heads...........255
12:37:25  Boot sector located at relative sector 63 (Cylinder 0, Head 1, Sector
1)
12:50:35  Boot sector located at relative sector 3084543 (Cylinder 192, Head 1,
Sector 1)
12:51:02  Boot sector located at relative sector 3196998 (Cylinder 199, Head 1,
Sector 1)
12:51:42  The whole-file CRC verifies:  22c1b141
12:52:40  Partition table for drive 0:
12:52:41  Restore of drive 0: to drive 0: completed on Nov 28, 2000 12:52
```

```
12:52:49  Menu selections:
            Function:              Restore
            Remote connection:     Local
            Direct access:         No
            Use XBIOS:             Auto
            Adjust partitions:     Auto
            Backfill on restore:   No
            Compress sector data:  Yes
          SafeBack execution ended on Nov 28, 2000 12:52.
```
Measure
10. after=hash(src)
```
A:\DISKHASH.EXE %Z% Version %I% Created %G% at %U%
Comment: beta5 hash F1 after DI-02,14,33,40,54,61
run start Tue Nov 28 15:03:27 2000
run finish Tue Nov 28 15:24:20 2000
drive 0x80 (master) no BIOS extensions
Disk SHA-1 hash 5FBEEB219E7282ED621645A67252A70F4D8BBF21
```
11. Compare(src,dst)
```
A:\ADJCMP.EXE @(#) Version 2.1 Created 10/10/00 at 15:36:36
Comment: beta2 DI-14 F1->D3(D:\F1T14)->D11
run start Tue Nov 28 12:57:38 2000
run finish Tue Nov 28 13:32:30 2000
3 partitions, Boot track sectors: compared 189 match 186 differ 3
Data track sectors: compared 3330243 match 3330237 differ 6
Data track sectors filled: zero 26273 src 3 dst 0 other 9285570 remaining 877
```
Output Specifications (expected results)
12. before=after
```
before = 5FBEEB219E7282ED621645A67252A70F4D8BBF21
after  = 5FBEEB219E7282ED621645A67252A70F4D8BBF21
```
13. src and dst compare adjusted equal
```
3 partitions, Boot track sectors: compared 189 match 186 differ 3
Data track sectors: compared 3330243 match 3330237 differ 6
```

Test case ID DI-15

Test assertions

9.   If a duplicate destination disk is created from an image file of a source disk with a smaller geometry and cylinder adjustment is not enabled, then the disks must compare equal.

10.   If a duplicate destination disk is created from an image file of a source disk with a smaller geometry, then the contents of the destination disk sectors not corresponding to source disk sectors must be as specified by the tool (if the tool allows such a specification). Otherwise each bit of such sectors must be set to zero.

28.   The source before using the tool must be equal to the source after tool use.

Setup
1. wipe(src)
```
A:\DISKWIPE.EXE @(#) Version 2.1 Created 09/27/00 at 13:44:51
Comment: Windows 98 setup
run start Wed Sep 27 17:40:45 2000
run finish Wed Sep 27 17:48:08 2000
drive 0x80 (master) no BIOS extensions
3330432 sectors wiped with F2
```
2. partition(src,1,*,Fat 32)
3. load_os(Windows 98)
```
Comment: beta5 F2 (W98) layout
```

```
Source disk partition table
P 000000063 001640961 0000/001/01 0406/063/63 Boot 0B Fat32
X 001641024 001689408 0407/000/01 0825/063/63      05 extended
S 000000063 001640961 0407/001/01 0813/063/63      0B Fat32
x 001641024 000048384 0814/000/01 0825/063/63      05 extended
S 000000063 000048321 0814/001/01 0825/063/63      04 Fat16
Source disk layout:  00826/064/63 3330432 total sectors on disk
      Start LBA    End LBA    Length    Size: MB   (binary)
  0 B         0         62         63     0.03MB    0.03BMB
  1 P        63    1641023    1640961   840.17MB  801.25BMB
  2 b   1641024    1641086         63     0.03MB    0.03BMB
  3 P   1641087    3282047    1640961   840.17MB  801.25BMB
  4 b   3282048    3282110         63     0.03MB    0.03BMB
  5 P   3282111    3330431      48321    24.74MB   23.59BMB
```

4. before=hash(src)

```
A:\DISKHASH.EXE @(#) Version 2.1 Created 09/27/00 at 13:44:51
Comment: reference hash for F2
run start Fri Sep 29 11:46:04 2000
run finish Fri Sep 29 12:49:43 2000
drive 0x80 (master) no BIOS extensions
Disk SHA-1 hash 96EDE9BC7D9A33A61A5537C5CB7DF45CAD6ED488
```

5. wipe(img)

6. partition(img,1,MAX,Big Fat 16)

7. wipe(dst)

```
A:\DISKWIPE.EXE @(#) Version 2.2 Created 10/02/00 at 09:08:26
Comment: beta5 wipe D11 for DI-15 F2->D3->D11
run start Tue Nov 14 10:37:39 2000
run finish Tue Nov 14 10:49:12 2000
drive 0x80 (master) no BIOS extensions
12643155 sectors wiped with DB
```

  Execute

8. image(src,img.1,f,n)

```
          SafeBack 2.0 31Jan00 execution started on Nov 14, 2000 11:21.
11:22:32  Menu selections:
              Function:              Backup
              Remote connection:     Local
              Direct access:         No
              Use XBIOS:             Auto
              Adjust partitions:     No
              Backfill on restore:   Yes
              Compress sector data:  Yes
11:24:37  Backup file F:\F2T15.001 created.
          Backup file comment record:
              Beta3 DI-15 F2->D3->D11  Fill, NO adjust
11:25:18  Backing up drive 0:
          to F:\F2T15.001 on Nov 14, 2000 11:25
11:25:19  Local SafeBack is running on DOS 6.30
          Source drive 0:
              Capacity........1628 MB
              Cylinders.......827
              Heads...........64
11:25:19  Partition table for drive 0:
11:37:15  Backup file CRC: 82d57464.
11:37:15  Backup of drive 0: completed on Nov 14, 2000 11:37.
          SafeBack execution ended on Nov 14, 2000 11:37.
```

9. load(img.1,dst)

```
          SafeBack 2.0 31Jan00 execution started on Nov 14, 2000 13:11.
13:11:24  Menu selections:
              Function:               Restore
              Remote connection:      Local
              Direct access:          No
              Use XBIOS:              Auto
              Adjust partitions:      No
              Backfill on restore:    Yes
              Compress sector data:   Yes
13:12:05  Backup file created on Nov 14, 2000 11:25
          by Gary Fisher Natl Institute of Standards & Technology Software
Diagnostics & Con
          Backup file comment record:
              Beta3 DI-15 F2->D3->D11  Fill, NO adjust
13:12:14  Backup file E:\F2T15.001 opened for access.
13:12:56  Restore of drive 0: from E:\F2T15.001
          to drive 0: started on Nov 14, 2000 13:12
13:12:56  Partition fixup has been disabled.
13:12:56  Local SafeBack is running on DOS 6.30
          Source drive 0:
              Capacity........1628 MB
              Cylinders.......827
              Heads...........64
          Destination drive 0:
              Capacity........6181 MB
              Cylinders.......788
              Heads...........255
13:27:04  The whole-file CRC verifies:  82d57464
13:38:52  Restore of drive 0: to drive 0: completed on Nov 14, 2000 13:38
13:42:32  Menu selections:
              Function:               Restore
              Remote connection:      Local
              Direct access:          No
              Use XBIOS:              Auto
              Adjust partitions:      No
              Backfill on restore:    Yes
              Compress sector data:   Yes
          SafeBack execution ended on Nov 14, 2000 13:42.
```

Measure

10. after=hash(src)

```
A:\DISKHASH.EXE @(#) Version 2.2 Created 10/02/00 at 09:08:26
Comment: beta5 hash F2 after DI-15
run start Tue Nov 14 13:43:06 2000
run finish Tue Nov 14 14:03:36 2000
drive 0x80 (master) no BIOS extensions
Disk SHA-1 hash 96EDE9BC7D9A33A61A5537C5CB7DF45CAD6ED488
```

11. Compare(src,dst)

```
A:\ADJCMP.EXE @(#) Version 2.1 Created 10/10/00 at 15:36:36
Comment: beta3 DI-15
run start Tue Nov 14 14:54:03 2000
run finish Tue Nov 14 15:22:57 2000
3 partitions, Boot track sectors: compared 189 match 189 differ 0
Data track sectors: compared 3330243 match 3330243 differ 0
Data track sectors filled: zero 9308691 src 0 dst 0 other 4032 remaining 0
```

Output Specifications (expected results)

12. before=after
```
before = 96EDE9BC7D9A33A61A5537C5CB7DF45CAD6ED488
after  = 96EDE9BC7D9A33A61A5537C5CB7DF45CAD6ED488
```
13. src and dst compare equal
```
3 partitions, Boot track sectors: compared 189 match 189 differ 0
Data track sectors: compared 3330243 match 3330243 differ 0
```
14. excess dst sectors zero filled
```
Data track sectors filled: zero 9308691 src 0 dst 0 other 4032 remaining 0
```

Test case ID DI-16 (Case not used)

Test assertions

7.   If a duplicate destination disk is created from an image file of a source disk with the same geometry, then the disks must compare equal.

28.   The source before using the tool must be equal to the source after tool use.

   Setup
1. wipe(src)
2. partition(src,1,*,NTFS)
3. partition(src,2,*,Fat 32)
4. load_os(Windows 2000)
5. before=hash(src)
6. wipe(img)
7. partition(img,1,MAX,Big Fat 16)
8. wipe(dst)
   Execute
9. image(src,img.1)
10. load(img.1,dst)
   Measure
11. after=hash(src)
12. Compare(src,dst)
   Output Specifications (expected results)
13. before=after
14. src and dst compare equal

Test case ID DI-17

Test assertions

7.   If a duplicate destination disk is created from an image file of a source disk with the same geometry, then the disks must compare equal.

23.   If the tool encounters any read errors while reading from the source, then the tool must detect and identify the error and notify the user.

27.   If the tool is able to create a destination from an image file that contains read errors, the destination sectors corresponding to the unreadable data must be treated as fill sectors (the tool may allow a specified action or may fill the sectors with zeros).

28.   The source before using the tool must be equal to the source after tool use.

   Setup
1. wipe(src)
```
A:\DISKWIPE.EXE @(#) Version 2.1 Created 09/27/00 at 13:44:51
Comment: initial setup for NT
run start Wed Sep 27 14:37:32 2000
```

```
run finish Wed Sep 27 14:44:44 2000
drive 0x80 (master) no BIOS extensions
3330432 sectors wiped with D9
```

2. partition(src,1,*,NTFS)

3. load_os(Windows NT)

```
Comment: beta5 D9 (NT) layout
Source disk partition table
P 000000063 003072321 0000/001/01 0761/063/63 Boot 07 NTFS
X 003072384 000262080 0762/000/01 0826/063/63      05 extended
S 000000063 000060417 0762/001/01 0776/063/63      07 NTFS
x 000060480 000080640 0777/000/01 0796/063/63      05 extended
S 000000063 000080577 0777/001/01 0796/063/63      07 NTFS
x 000141120 000120960 0797/000/01 0826/063/63      05 extended
S 000000063 000120897 0797/001/01 0826/063/63      07 NTFS
Source disk layout:  00826/064/63 3330432 total sectors on disk
     Start LBA    End LBA    Length    Size: MB    (binary)
 0 B         0         62        63     0.03MB     0.03BMB
 1 P        63    3072383   3072321  1573.03MB  1500.16BMB
 2 b   3072384    3072446        63     0.03MB     0.03BMB
 3 P   3072447    3132863     60417    30.93MB    29.50BMB
 4 b   3132864    3132926        63     0.03MB     0.03BMB
 5 P   3132927    3213503     80577    41.26MB    39.34BMB
 6 b   3213504    3213566        63     0.03MB     0.03BMB
 7 P   3213567    3334463    120897    61.90MB    59.03BMB
```

4. before=hash(src)

```
A:\DISKHASH.EXE @(#) Version 2.1 Created 09/27/00 at 13:44:51
Comment: Reference hash on D9 (NTFS)
run start Fri Sep 29 11:21:28 2000
run finish Fri Sep 29 12:26:11 2000
drive 0x80 (master) no BIOS extensions
Disk SHA-1 hash A683672031589F08895F3AEDE8DBC77718648284
```

5. wipe(img)

6. partition(img,1,MAX,Big Fat 16)

7. wipe(dst)

```
A:\DISKWIPE.EXE @(#) Version 2.2 Created 10/02/00 at 09:08:26
Comment: Beta5 wipe D2 for DI-17 (D9->D3->D2)
run start Mon Nov 13 17:35:42 2000
run finish Mon Nov 13 17:45:34 2000
drive 0x80 (master) no BIOS extensions
3330432 sectors wiped with D2
```

Execute

8. baddisk(src,read)

```
return code 00010 on command 00002 from disk 00128 (00063 Max head value)
at address 00127/00063/00063
baddisk  compiled on 11/03/00 at 09:12:12
@(#) Version 1.1 Created 11/03/00 at 09:11:04
return code 00010 on command 00010 from disk 00128 (00063 Max head value)
at address 00127/00063/00063
baddisk  compiled on 11/03/00 at 09:12:12
@(#) Version 1.1 Created 11/03/00 at 09:11:04
```

9. image(src,img.1)

```
        SafeBack 2.0 31Jan00 execution started on Nov 14, 2000 10:13.
10:14:13  Menu selections:
          Function:            Backup
          Remote connection:   Local
          Direct access:       No
```

```
              Use XBIOS:              Auto
              Adjust partitions:      Auto
              Backfill on restore:    Yes
              Compress sector data:   Yes
10:16:55   Backup file C:\D9T17.001 created.
           Backup file comment record:
              Test DI-17 D9->D3:C->D2
10:17:26   Backing up drive 0:
              to C:\D9T17.001 on Nov 14, 2000 10:17
10:17:28   Local SafeBack is running on DOS 6.30
           Source drive 0:
              Capacity........1628 MB
              Cylinders.......827
              Heads...........64
10:17:28   Partition table for drive 0:
10:19:11   While reading drive 0: a sector flagged bad error (status 0a)
occurred:
              at relative sector 516095 (Cylinder 127, Head 63, Sector 63)
10:29:24   Backup file CRC: 6061bd9c.
10:29:24   Backup of drive 0: completed on Nov 14, 2000 10:29.
           SafeBack execution ended on Nov 14, 2000 10:30.
```

10. load(img.1,dst)

```
           SafeBack 2.0 31Jan00 execution started on Nov 14, 2000 10:48.
10:48:12   Menu selections:
              Function:               Restore
              Remote connection:      Local
              Direct access:          No
              Use XBIOS:              Auto
              Adjust partitions:      Auto
              Backfill on restore:    Yes
              Compress sector data:   Yes
10:48:30   Backup file created on Nov 14, 2000 10:17
           by Gary Fisher Natl Institute of Standards & Technology Software
Diagnostics & Con
           Backup file comment record:
              Test DI-17 D9->D3:C->D2
10:48:34   Backup file C:\D9T17.001 opened for access.
10:48:55   Restore of drive 0: from C:\D9T17.001
              to drive 0: started on Nov 14, 2000 10:48
10:48:55   Local SafeBack is running on DOS 6.30
           Source drive 0:
              Capacity........1628 MB
              Cylinders.......827
              Heads...........64
           Destination drive 0:
              Capacity........1628 MB
              Cylinders.......827
              Heads...........64
10:51:08   The image for 0: shows that a sector flagged bad error (status 0a)
occurred
              during backup at relative sector 516095 (Cylinder 127, Head 63, Sector
63)
11:03:20   The whole-file CRC verifies:  6061bd9c
11:03:20   Partition table for drive 0:
11:03:22   Restore of drive 0: to drive 0: completed on Nov 14, 2000 11:03
11:03:32   Menu selections:
              Function:               Restore
              Remote connection:      Local
```

```
        Direct access:        No
        Use XBIOS:            Auto
        Adjust partitions:    Auto
        Backfill on restore:  Yes
        Compress sector data: Yes
        SafeBack execution ended on Nov 14, 2000 11:03.
```

Measure

11. after=hash(src)

```
A:\DISKHASH.EXE @(#) Version 2.2 Created 10/02/00 at 09:08:26
Comment: beta5 hash after DI-17 (D9)
run start Tue Nov 14 11:10:48 2000
run finish Tue Nov 14 11:34:47 2000
drive 0x80 (master) no BIOS extensions
Disk SHA-1 hash A683672031589F08895F3AEDE8DBC77718648284
```

12. Examine_message(I/O error)

```
10:19:11  While reading drive 0: a sector flagged bad error (status 0a)
occurred:
10:51:08  The image for 0: shows that a sector flagged bad error (status 0a)
occurred
11:03:20  The whole-file CRC verifies:  6061bd9c
```

13. Compare(src,dst)

```
Comment: beta2 DI-17 D2->D3->D9
run start Tue Nov 14 11:43:41 2000
run finish Tue Nov 14 11:55:05 2000
sectors compared 3330432 match 3330431 differ 1 dropped 0
filled: zero 0 src 0 dst 0 other 0 remainder 0
```

Output Specifications (expected results)

14. before=after

```
before = A683672031589F08895F3AEDE8DBC77718648284
after  = A683672031589F08895F3AEDE8DBC77718648284
```

15. I/O error message

```
10:19:11  While reading drive 0: a sector flagged bad error (status 0a)
occurred:
10:51:08  The image for 0: shows that a sector flagged bad error (status 0a)
occurred
11:03:20  The whole-file CRC verifies:  6061bd9c
```

16. src and dst compare qualified equal

```
sectors compared 3330432 match 3330431 differ 1 dropped 0
```

Test case ID DI-18

Test assertions

8. *If a duplicate destination disk is created from an image file of a source disk with a smaller geometry and cylinder adjustment is enabled, then the disks must compare adjusted equal.*

10. *If a duplicate destination disk is created from an image file of a source disk with a smaller geometry, then the contents of the destination disk sectors not corresponding to source disk sectors must be as specified by the tool (if the tool allows such a specification). Otherwise each bit of such sectors must be set to zero.*

26. *If the tool encounters any write errors while writing to the destination, then the tool must detect and identify the error and notify the user.*

28. *The source before using the tool must be equal to the source after tool use.*

Setup

1. wipe(src)

```
A:\DISKWIPE.EXE @(#) Version 2.1 Created 09/27/00 at 13:44:51
```

```
Comment: Linux setup
run start Thu Sep 28 14:49:16 2000
run finish Thu Sep 28 14:56:29 2000
drive 0x80 (master) no BIOS extensions
3330432 sectors wiped with D4
```

2. partition(src,1,*,Linux)
3. partition(src,2,*,Linux Swap)
4. load_os(Linux)

```
Comment: D4 (linux) layout
Source disk partition table
P 000000063 002048193 0000/001/01 0507/063/63 Boot 83 Linux
X 002048256 001286208 0508/000/01 0826/063/63      05 extended
S 000000063 000205569 0508/001/01 0558/063/63      82 Linux swap
x 000205632 001080576 0559/000/01 0826/063/63      05 extended
S 000000063 001080513 0559/001/01 0826/063/63      83 Linux
Source disk layout:   00826/064/63 3330432 total sectors on disk
        Start LBA    End LBA    Length    Size: MB    (binary)
  0 B          0         62        63     0.03MB      0.03BMB
  1 P         63    2048255   2048193  1048.67MB   1000.09BMB
  2 b    2048256    2048318        63     0.03MB      0.03BMB
  3 P    2048319    2253887    205569   105.25MB    100.38BMB
  4 b    2253888    2253950        63     0.03MB      0.03BMB
  5 P    2253951    3334463   1080513   553.22MB    527.59BMB
```

5. before=hash(src)

```
A:\DISKHASH.EXE @(#) Version 2.2 Created 10/02/00 at 09:08:26
Comment: beta5, hash d4 for test DI-12
run start Thu Oct 12 08:39:28 2000
run finish Thu Oct 12 08:59:54 2000
drive 0x80 (master) no BIOS extensions
Disk SHA-1 hash D25C035B74F3EECFCBA4A1968AA6D48096D92EE2
```

6. wipe(img)
7. partition(img,1,MAX,Big Fat 16)
8. wipe(dst)

```
A:\DISKWIPE.EXE @(#) Version 2.2 Created 10/02/00 at 09:08:26
Comment: beta5 DI-18
run start Tue Nov 14 17:11:52 2000
run finish Tue Nov 14 17:23:25 2000
drive 0x80 (master) no BIOS extensions
12643155 sectors wiped with DB
```

   Execute

9. image(src,img.1,f,a)

```
          SafeBack 2.0 31Jan00 execution started on Nov 14, 2000 17:07.
17:07:28  Menu selections:
              Function:              Backup
              Remote connection:     Local
              Direct access:         No
              Use XBIOS:             Auto
              Adjust partitions:     Auto
              Backfill on restore:   Yes
              Compress sector data:  Yes
17:08:09  Backup file F:\D4T18.001 created.
          Backup file comment record:
              beta3 DI-18
17:08:50  Backing up drive 0:
          to F:\D4T18.001 on Nov 14, 2000 17:08
```

```
17:08:52   Local SafeBack is running on DOS 6.30
           Source drive 0:
             Capacity........1628 MB
             Cylinders.......827
             Heads...........64
17:08:52   Partition table for drive 0:
17:20:35   Backup file CRC: f0066c85.
17:20:35   Backup of drive 0: completed on Nov 14, 2000 17:20.
           SafeBack execution ended on Nov 14, 2000 17:20.
```

10. baddisk(dst,write)

```
return code 00010 on command 00003 from disk 00128 (00254 Max head value)
at address 00600/00100/00002
baddisk  compiled on 11/03/00 at 09:12:12
@(#) Version 1.1 Created 11/03/00 at 09:11:04
return code 00010 on command 00003 from disk 00128 (00254 Max head value)
at address 00100/00005/00025
baddisk  compiled on 11/03/00 at 09:12:12
@(#) Version 1.1 Created 11/03/00 at 09:11:04
```

11. load(img.1,dst)

```
           SafeBack 2.0 31Jan00 execution started on Nov 14, 2000 17:34.
17:34:32   Menu selections:
             Function:               Restore
             Remote connection:      Local
             Direct access:          No
             Use XBIOS:              Auto
             Adjust partitions:      Auto
             Backfill on restore:    Yes
             Compress sector data:   Yes
17:34:54   Backup file created on Nov 14, 2000 17:08
           by Gary Fisher Natl Institute of Standards & Technology Software
Diagnostics & Con
           Backup file comment record:
             beta3 DI-18
17:35:00   Backup file F:\D4T18.001 opened for access.
17:35:21   Restore of drive 0: from F:\D4T18.001
           to drive 0: started on Nov 14, 2000 17:35
17:35:21   Local SafeBack is running on DOS 6.30
           Source drive 0:
             Capacity........1628 MB
             Cylinders.......827
             Heads...........64
           Destination drive 0:
             Capacity........6181 MB
             Cylinders.......788
             Heads...........255
17:35:22   Boot sector located at relative sector 63 (Cylinder 0, Head 1, Sector
1)
17:41:49   While writing drive 0:, a sector flagged bad error (status 0a)
occurred
           at relative sector 1606839 (Cylinder 100, Head 5, Sector 25)
17:43:34   Boot sector located at relative sector 2056383 (Cylinder 128, Head 1,
Sector 1)
17:44:26   Boot sector located at relative sector 2265228 (Cylinder 141, Head 1,
Sector 1)
17:49:02   The whole-file CRC verifies:   f0066c85
17:50:57   Partition table for drive 0:
```

```
17:58:57   While writing drive 0:, a sector flagged bad error (status 0a)
occurred
           at relative sector 9645301 (Cylinder 600, Head 100, Sector 2)
18:02:48   Restore of drive 0: to drive 0: completed on Nov 14, 2000 18:02
18:03:04   Menu selections:
              Function:                Restore
              Remote connection:       Local
              Direct access:           No
              Use XBIOS:               Auto
              Adjust partitions:       Auto
              Backfill on restore:     Yes
              Compress sector data:    Yes
           SafeBack execution ended on Nov 14, 2000 18:03.
```

Measure

12. after=hash(src)

```
A:\DISKHASH.EXE @(#) Version 2.2 Created 10/02/00 at 09:08:26
Comment: Hash D4 on beta5 after DI-18
run start Tue Nov 14 17:27:10 2000
run finish Tue Nov 14 17:47:45 2000
drive 0x80 (master) no BIOS extensions
Disk SHA-1 hash D25C035B74F3EECFCBA4A1968AA6D48096D92EE2
```

13. Examine_message(I/O error)

```
17:41:49   While writing drive 0:, a sector flagged bad error (status 0a)
occurred
17:49:02   The whole-file CRC verifies:   f0066c85
17:58:57   While writing drive 0:, a sector flagged bad error (status 0a)
occurred
```

14. Compare(src,dst)

```
A:\ADJCMP.EXE @(#) Version 2.1 Created 10/10/00 at 15:36:36
Comment: Beta3 DI-18 write errors on dst at 100/5/25 & 600/100/2
run start Tue Nov 14 18:29:03 2000
run finish Tue Nov 14 18:58:00 2000
3 partitions, Boot track sectors: compared 189 match 186 differ 3
Data track sectors: compared 3334275 match 3334254 differ 21
Data track sectors filled: zero 9307939 src 2 dst 1 other 1 remaining 748
```

Output Specifications (expected results)

15. before=after

```
before = D25C035B74F3EECFCBA4A1968AA6D48096D92EE2
after  = D25C035B74F3EECFCBA4A1968AA6D48096D92EE2
```

16. I/O error message

```
17:41:49   While writing drive 0:, a sector flagged bad error (status 0a)
occurred
17:49:02   The whole-file CRC verifies:   f0066c85
17:58:57   While writing drive 0:, a sector flagged bad error (status 0a)
occurred
```

17. src and dst compare qualified equal

```
3 partitions, Boot track sectors: compared 189 match 186 differ 3
Data track sectors: compared 3334275 match 3334254 differ 21
```

18. excess dst sectors zero filled

```
Data track sectors filled: zero 9307939 src 2 dst 1 other 1 remaining 748
```

Test case ID DI-21

Test assertions

7. *If a duplicate destination disk is created from an image file of a source disk with the same geometry, then the disks must compare equal.*

28. *The source before using the tool must be equal to the source after tool use.*

29. *The results of any remote tool use must be equal to the results of local identical tool use.*

Setup

1. wipe(src)

```
A:\DISKWIPE.EXE @(#) Version 2.1 Created 09/27/00 at 13:44:51
Comment: DOS Setup
run start Wed Sep 27 17:47:09 2000
run finish Wed Sep 27 17:54:19 2000
drive 0x80 (master) no BIOS extensions
3330432 sectors wiped with D1
```

2. partition(src,1,*,Fat 12)

3. partition(src,2,*,Small Fat 16)

4. load_os(DOS)

```
Comment: beta5 D1 (DOS) Layout
Source disk partition table
P 000000063 000024129 0000/001/01 0005/063/63 Boot 01 Fat12
X 000024192 003306240 0006/000/01 0825/063/63      05 extended
S 000000063 000044289 0006/001/01 0016/063/63      04 Fat16
x 000044352 003261888 0017/000/01 0825/063/63      05 extended
S 000000063 003261825 0017/001/01 0825/063/63      06 Fat16
Source disk layout:  00826/064/63 3330432 total sectors on disk
      Start LBA    End LBA    Length    Size: MB   (binary)
  0 B         0         62        63     0.03MB    0.03BMB
  1 P        63      24191     24129    12.35MB   11.78BMB
  2 b     24192      24254        63     0.03MB    0.03BMB
  3 P     24255      68543     44289    22.68MB   21.63BMB
  4 b     68544      68606        63     0.03MB    0.03BMB
  5 P     68607    3330431   3261825  1670.05MB 1592.69BMB
```

5. before=hash(src)

```
A:\DISKHASH.EXE @(#) Version 2.1 Created 09/27/00 at 13:44:51
Comment: hash D1 before running SafeBack
run start Fri Sep 29 11:06:09 2000
run finish Fri Sep 29 12:09:44 2000
drive 0x80 (master) no BIOS extensions
Disk SHA-1 hash 305B31403D8AD36BCB9AF108821818DCFA3F919A
```

6. wipe(img)

7. partition(img,1,MAX,Big Fat 16)

8. wipe(dst)

```
A:\DISKWIPE.EXE @(#) Version 2.2 Created 10/02/00 at 09:08:26
Comment: beta5 DI-21 wipe D2
run start Mon Nov 20 10:53:10 2000
run finish Mon Nov 20 11:00:16 2000
drive 0x80 (master) no BIOS extensions
3330432 sectors wiped with D2
```

Execute

9. establish_link()

10. image(src,img.1)

```
        SafeBack 2.0 31Jan00 execution started on Nov 19, 2000 11:55.
```

```
11:56:03  Menu selections:
                  Function:                  Backup
                  Remote connection:         LPT1:
                  Direct access:             No
                  Use XBIOS:                 Auto
                  Adjust partitions:         Auto
                  Backfill on restore:       Yes
                  Compress sector data:      Yes
11:56:34  Backup file C:\D1T21.001 created.
          Backup file comment record:
                  Backup of D1 to D3 C:\D1T21 Beta3->Beta2
11:57:34  Backing up drive 0:
          to C:\D1T21.001 on Nov 19, 2000 11:57
11:57:36  Local SafeBack is running on DOS 6.30
11:57:36  Remote SafeBack server is running on DOS 6.30
          Source drive 0:
                  Capacity........1628 MB
                  Cylinders.......827
                  Heads..........64
11:57:36  Partition table for drive 0:
19:58:18  Backup file CRC: 8d763fdc.
19:58:18  Backup of drive 0: completed on Nov 19, 2000 19:58.
          SafeBack execution ended on Nov 20, 2000 10:21.
```

11. load(img.1,dst)

```
          SafeBack 2.0 31Jan00 execution started on Nov 20, 2000 11:04.
11:04:06  Menu selections:
                  Function:                  Restore
                  Remote connection:         Local
                  Direct access:             No
                  Use XBIOS:                 Auto
                  Adjust partitions:         Auto
                  Backfill on restore:       Yes
                  Compress sector data:      Yes
11:04:19  Backup file created on Nov 19, 2000 11:57
          by Gary Fisher Natl Institute of Standards & Technology Software
Diagnostics & Con
          Backup file comment record:
                  Backup of D1 to D3 C:\D1T21 Beta3->Beta2
11:04:22  Backup file C:\D1T21.001 opened for access.
11:04:41  Restore of drive 0: from C:\D1T21.001
          to drive 1: started on Nov 20, 2000 11:04
11:04:41  Local SafeBack is running on DOS 6.30
          Source drive 0:
                  Capacity........1628 MB
                  Cylinders.......827
                  Heads..........64
          Destination drive 1:
                  Capacity........1628 MB
                  Cylinders.......827
                  Heads..........64
11:15:42  The whole-file CRC verifies:  8d763fdc
11:15:42  Partition table for drive 1:
11:15:44  Restore of drive 0: to drive 1: completed on Nov 20, 2000 11:15
11:24:22  Menu selections:
                  Function:                  Restore
                  Remote connection:         Local
                  Direct access:             No
                  Use XBIOS:                 Auto
```

```
        Adjust partitions:      Auto
        Backfill on restore:    Yes
        Compress sector data:   Yes
        SafeBack execution ended on Nov 20, 2000 11:24.
```

Measure

12. after=hash(src)

```
A:\DISKHASH.EXE @(#) Version 2.2 Created 10/02/00 at 09:08:26
Comment: beta5 hash disk after DI-21
run start Mon Nov 20 11:41:49 2000
run finish Mon Nov 20 12:02:03 2000
drive 0x80 (master) no BIOS extensions
Disk SHA-1 hash 305B31403D8AD36BCB9AF108821818DCFA3F919A
```

13. Compare(src,dst)

```
Comment: beta2 DI-21
run start Mon Nov 20 11:26:42 2000
run finish Mon Nov 20 11:37:54 2000
sectors compared 3330432 match 3330432 differ 0 dropped 0
filled: zero 0 src 0 dst 0 other 0 remainder 0
```

Output Specifications (expected results)

14. before=after

```
before = 305B31403D8AD36BCB9AF108821818DCFA3F919A
after  = 305B31403D8AD36BCB9AF108821818DCFA3F919A
```

15. src and dst compare equal

```
sectors compared 3330432 match 3330432 differ 0 dropped 0
```

Test case ID DI-22

Test assertions

9.   If a duplicate destination disk is created from an image file of a source disk with a smaller geometry and cylinder adjustment is not enabled, then the disks must compare equal.

10.   If a duplicate destination disk is created from an image file of a source disk with a smaller geometry, then the contents of the destination disk sectors not corresponding to source disk sectors must be as specified by the tool (if the tool allows such a specification). Otherwise each bit of such sectors must be set to zero.

23.   If the tool encounters any read errors while reading from the source, then the tool must detect and identify the error and notify the user.

27.   If the tool is able to create a destination from an image file that contains read errors, the destination sectors corresponding to the unreadable data must be treated as fill sectors (the tool may allow a specified action or may fill the sectors with zeros).

28.   The source before using the tool must be equal to the source after tool use.

29.   The results of any remote tool use must be equal to the results of local identical tool use.

Setup

1. wipe(src)

```
A:\DISKWIPE.EXE @(#) Version 2.1 Created 09/27/00 at 13:44:51
Comment: Windows 95 setup
run start Wed Sep 27 17:52:35 2000
run finish Wed Sep 27 17:59:47 2000
drive 0x80 (master) no BIOS extensions
3330432 sectors wiped with F1
```

2. partition(src,1,*,Big Fat 16)

3. load_os(Windows 95)

```
Comment: beta5 F1 W95 layout
Source disk partition table
```

```
P 000000063 003072321 0000/001/01 0761/063/63 Boot 06 Fat16
X 003072384 000258048 0762/000/01 0825/063/63      05 extended
S 000000063 000104769 0762/001/01 0787/063/63      06 Fat16
x 000104832 000153216 0788/000/01 0825/063/63      05 extended
S 000000063 000153153 0788/001/01 0825/063/63      06 Fat16
Source disk layout:  00826/064/63 3330432 total sectors on disk
        Start LBA    End LBA    Length    Size: MB   (binary)
   0 B          0         62        63     0.03MB     0.03MB
   1 P         63    3072383   3072321  1573.03MB  1500.16BMB
   2 b    3072384    3072446        63     0.03MB     0.03BMB
   3 P    3072447    3177215    104769    53.64MB    51.16BMB
   4 b    3177216    3177278        63     0.03MB     0.03BMB
   5 P    3177279    3330431    153153    78.41MB    74.78BMB
```

4. before=hash(src)

```
A:\DISKHASH.EXE @(#) Version 2.2 Created 10/02/00 at 09:08:26
Comment: rehash F1 (Win 95)
run start Fri Nov 03 14:08:19 2000
run finish Fri Nov 03 14:28:46 2000
drive 0x80 (master) no BIOS extensions
Disk SHA-1 hash 5FBEEB219E7282ED621645A67252A70F4D8BBF21
```

5. wipe(img)

6. partition(img,1,MAX,Big Fat 16)

7. wipe(dst)

```
A:\DISKWIPE.EXE @(#) Version 2.2 Created 10/02/00 at 09:08:26
Comment: beta5 wipe D11 for DI-22
run start Tue Nov 21 12:04:35 2000
run finish Tue Nov 21 12:16:11 2000
drive 0x80 (master) no BIOS extensions
12643155 sectors wiped with DB
```

  Execute

8. establish_link()

9. baddisk(src,read)

```
return code 00010 on command 00002 from disk 00128 (00063 Max head value)
at address 00003/00011/00049
baddisk  compiled on 11/03/00 at 09:12:12
@(#) Version 1.1 Created 11/03/00 at 09:11:04
return code 00010 on command 00010 from disk 00128 (00063 Max head value)
at address 00003/00011/00049
baddisk  compiled on 11/03/00 at 09:12:12
@(#) Version 1.1 Created 11/03/00 at 09:11:04
```

10. image(src,img.1,n,n)

```
          SafeBack 2.0 31Jan00 execution started on Nov 20, 2000 17:28.
17:29:23  Menu selections:
              Function:              Backup
              Remote connection:     LPT1:
              Direct access:         No
              Use XBIOS:             Auto
              Adjust partitions:     No
              Backfill on restore:   No
              Compress sector data:  Yes
17:30:02  Backup file F:\F1T22.001 created.
          Backup file comment record:
            DI-22 Beta2:F1->Beta3:D3 (F:\F1T22)->D11
17:31:29  Backing up drive 0:
            to F:\F1T22.001 on Nov 20, 2000 17:31
17:31:31  Local SafeBack is running on DOS 6.30
```

```
17:31:31   Remote SafeBack server is running on DOS 6.30
           Source drive 0:
              Capacity........1628 MB
              Cylinders.......827
              Heads..........64
17:31:31   Partition table for drive 0:
17:33:20   While reading drive 0: a sector flagged bad error (status 0a)
occurred:
           at relative sector 12837 (Cylinder 3, Head 11, Sector 49)
02:10:57   Backup file CRC: 5ad5b572.
02:10:57   Backup of drive 0: completed on Nov 21, 2000 02:10.
           SafeBack execution ended on Nov 21, 2000 10:23.
```

11. load(img.1,dst)

```
           SafeBack 2.0 31Jan00 execution started on Nov 21, 2000 12:34.
12:34:30   Menu selections:
              Function:             Restore
              Remote connection:    Local
              Direct access:        No
              Use XBIOS:            Auto
              Adjust partitions:    No
              Backfill on restore:  No
              Compress sector data: Yes
12:34:50   Backup file created on Nov 20, 2000 17:31
           by Gary Fisher Natl Institute of Standards & Technology Software
Diagnostics & Con
           Backup file comment record:
              DI-22 Beta2:F1->Beta3:D3 (F:\F1T22)->D11
12:34:55   Backup file F:\F1T22.001 opened for access.
12:35:11   Restore of drive 0: from F:\F1T22.001
           to drive 0: started on Nov 21, 2000 12:35
12:35:11   Partition fixup has been disabled.
12:35:11   Local SafeBack is running on DOS 6.30
           Source drive 0:
              Capacity........1628 MB
              Cylinders.......827
              Heads..........64
           Destination drive 0:
              Capacity........6181 MB
              Cylinders.......788
              Heads..........255
12:35:15   The image for 0: shows that a sector flagged bad error (status 0a)
occurred
           during backup at relative sector 12837 (Cylinder 3, Head 11, Sector
49)
12:49:15   The whole-file CRC verifies:  5ad5b572
13:31:02   Restore of drive 0: to drive 0: completed on Nov 21, 2000 13:31
13:45:57   Menu selections:
              Function:             Restore
              Remote connection:    Local
              Direct access:        No
              Use XBIOS:            Auto
              Adjust partitions:    No
              Backfill on restore:  No
              Compress sector data: Yes
           SafeBack execution ended on Nov 21, 2000 13:46.
```

Measure

12. after=hash(src)
```
A:\DISKHASH.EXE @(#) Version 2.2 Created 10/02/00 at 09:08:26
Comment: beta5 DI-22
run start Tue Nov 21 14:29:13 2000
run finish Tue Nov 21 14:49:40 2000
drive 0x80 (master) no BIOS extensions
Disk SHA-1 hash 5FBEEB219E7282ED621645A67252A70F4D8BBF21
```
13. Examine_message(I/O error)
```
17:33:20  While reading drive 0: a sector flagged bad error (status 0a)
occurred:
12:35:15  The image for 0: shows that a sector flagged bad error (status 0a)
occurred
12:49:15  The whole-file CRC verifies:  5ad5b572
```
14. Compare(src,dst)
```
Comment: DI-22 beta2 F1->D3 (F:\F1T22)->D11
run start Tue Nov 21 13:52:41 2000
run finish Tue Nov 21 14:22:48 2000
sectors compared 3330432 match 3330431 differ 1 dropped 0
filled: zero 9308691 src 0  dst 0  other 4032 remainder 0
```
   Output Specifications (expected results)
15. before=after
```
before = 5FBEEB219E7282ED621645A67252A70F4D8BBF21
after  = 5FBEEB219E7282ED621645A67252A70F4D8BBF21
```
16. I/O error message
```
17:33:20  While reading drive 0: a sector flagged bad error (status 0a)
occurred:
12:35:15  The image for 0: shows that a sector flagged bad error (status 0a)
occurred
12:49:15  The whole-file CRC verifies:  5ad5b572
```
17. src and dst compare qualified equal
```
sectors compared 3330432 match 3330431 differ 1 dropped 0
```

Test case ID DI-23

Test assertions

7.   If a duplicate destination disk is created from an image file of a source disk with the same geometry, then the disks must compare equal.

25.   If the tool encounters any write errors while creating an image file, then the tool must detect and identify the error and notify the user.

28.   The source before using the tool must be equal to the source after tool use.

   Setup

1. wipe(src)
```
A:\DISKWIPE.EXE @(#) Version 2.1 Created 09/27/00 at 13:44:51
Comment: initial setup for NT
run start Wed Sep 27 14:37:32 2000
run finish Wed Sep 27 14:44:44 2000
drive 0x80 (master) no BIOS extensions
3330432 sectors wiped with D9
```
2. partition(src,1,*,NTFS)

3. load_os(Windows NT)
```
Comment: beta5 D9 (NT) layout
Source disk partition table
P 000000063 003072321 0000/001/01 0761/063/63 Boot 07 NTFS
X 003072384 000262080 0762/000/01 0826/063/63     05 extended
```

60

```
S 000000063 000060417 0762/001/01 0776/063/63     07 NTFS
x 000060480 000080640 0777/000/01 0796/063/63     05 extended
S 000000063 000080577 0777/001/01 0796/063/63     07 NTFS
x 000141120 000120960 0797/000/01 0826/063/63     05 extended
S 000000063 000120897 0797/001/01 0826/063/63     07 NTFS
Source disk layout: 00826/064/63 3330432 total sectors on disk
      Start LBA   End LBA   Length   Size: MB   (binary)
  0 B        0        62       63     0.03MB     0.03BMB
  1 P       63   3072383  3072321  1573.03MB  1500.16BMB
  2 b  3072384   3072446       63     0.03MB     0.03BMB
  3 P  3072447   3132863    60417    30.93MB    29.50BMB
  4 b  3132864   3132926       63     0.03MB     0.03BMB
  5 P  3132927   3213503    80577    41.26MB    39.34BMB
  6 b  3213504   3213566       63     0.03MB     0.03BMB
  7 P  3213567   3334463   120897    61.90MB    59.03BMB
```

4. before=hash(src)

```
A:\DISKHASH.EXE @(#) Version 2.1 Created 09/27/00 at 13:44:51
Comment: Reference hash on D9 (NTFS)
run start Fri Sep 29 11:21:28 2000
run finish Fri Sep 29 12:26:11 2000
drive 0x80 (master) no BIOS extensions
Disk SHA-1 hash A683672031589F08895F3AEDE8DBC77718648284
```

5. wipe(img)

6. partition(img,1,MAX,Big Fat 16)

7. wipe(dst)

   Execute

8. baddisk(img,write)

```
return code 00010 on command 00003 from disk 00129 (00254 Max head value)
at address 00396/00121/00037
baddisk  compiled on 11/03/00 at 09:12:12
@(#) Version 1.1 Created 11/03/00 at 09:11:04
```

9. image(src,img.1)

```
        SafeBack 2.0 31Jan00 execution started on Nov 20, 2000 14:45.
14:46:25 Menu selections:
            Function:            Backup
            Remote connection:   Local
            Direct access:       No
            Use XBIOS:           Auto
            Adjust partitions:   Auto
            Backfill on restore: Yes
            Compress sector data: Yes
14:47:09 Backup file E:\D9T23.001 created.
         Backup file comment record:
            DI-23 on Beta2 write error @ 396/121/37 D9->D3(E:\D9T23)->D2
14:48:14 Backing up drive 0:
         to E:\D9T23.001 on Nov 20, 2000 14:48
14:48:14 Local SafeBack is running on DOS 6.30
         Source drive 0:
            Capacity........1628 MB
            Cylinders.......827
            Heads...........64
14:48:14 Partition table for drive 0:
14:55:18 An unrecoverable file error was reported while writing backup
         file D9T23.001.  The session is terminated.
15:03:01 Backup terminated by user or error on Nov 20, 2000 15:03.
```

```
15:03:11  Backup file deleted.
          SafeBack execution ended on Nov 20, 2000 15:03.
```
10. load(img.1,dst)

   Measure

11. after=hash(src)
```
A:\DISKHASH.EXE @(#) Version 2.2 Created 10/02/00 at 09:08:26
Comment: beta5 DI-23
run start Mon Nov 20 15:08:28 2000
run finish Mon Nov 20 15:28:55 2000
drive 0x80 (master) no BIOS extensions
Disk SHA-1 hash A683672031589F08895F3AEDE8DBC77718648284
```
12. Examine_message(I/O error)

13. Compare(src,dst)

   Output Specifications (expected results)

14. before=after
```
before = A683672031589F08895F3AEDE8DBC77718648284
after  = A683672031589F08895F3AEDE8DBC77718648284
```
15. I/O error message

16. src and dst compare qualified equal

Test case ID DI-24

Test assertions

7.   If a duplicate destination disk is created from an image file of a source disk with the same geometry, then the disks must compare equal.

24.   If the tool encounters any read errors while reading from an image file, then the tool must detect and identify the error and notify the user.

27.   If the tool is able to create a destination from an image file that contains read errors, the destination sectors corresponding to the unreadable data must be treated as fill sectors (the tool may allow a specified action or may fill the sectors with zeros).

28.   The source before using the tool must be equal to the source after tool use.

   Setup

1. wipe(src)
```
A:\DISKWIPE.EXE @(#) Version 2.1 Created 09/27/00 at 13:44:51
Comment: Windows 98 setup
run start Wed Sep 27 17:40:45 2000
run finish Wed Sep 27 17:48:08 2000
drive 0x80 (master) no BIOS extensions
3330432 sectors wiped with F2
```
2. partition(src,1,*,Fat 32)

3. load_os(Windows 98)
```
Comment: beta5 F2 (W98) layout
Source disk partition table
P 000000063 001640961 0000/001/01 0406/063/63 Boot 0B Fat32
X 001641024 001689408 0407/000/01 0825/063/63      05 extended
S 000000063 001640961 0407/001/01 0813/063/63      0B Fat32
x 001641024 000048384 0814/000/01 0825/063/63      05 extended
S 000000063 000048321 0814/001/01 0825/063/63      04 Fat16
Source disk layout:  00826/064/63 3330432 total sectors on disk
     Start LBA   End LBA    Length   Size: MB   (binary)
 0 B        0        62        63     0.03MB     0.03BMB
 1 P       63   1641023   1640961   840.17MB   801.25BMB
 2 b  1641024   1641086        63     0.03MB     0.03BMB
```

62

```
3  P    1641087   3282047   1640961   840.17MB   801.25BMB
4  b    3282048   3282110        63     0.03MB     0.03BMB
5  P    3282111   3330431     48321    24.74MB    23.59BMB
```

4. before=hash(src)

```
A:\DISKHASH.EXE @(#) Version 2.1 Created 09/27/00 at 13:44:51
Comment: reference hash for F2
run start Fri Sep 29 11:46:04 2000
run finish Fri Sep 29 12:49:43 2000
drive 0x80 (master) no BIOS extensions
Disk SHA-1 hash 96EDE9BC7D9A33A61A5537C5CB7DF45CAD6ED488
```

5. wipe(img)

6. partition(img,1,MAX,Big Fat 16)

7. wipe(dst)

```
A:\DISKWIPE.EXE @(#) Version 2.2 Created 10/02/00 at 09:08:26
Comment: beta5 setup for DI-24
run start Tue Nov 14 15:01:48 2000
run finish Tue Nov 14 15:09:22 2000
drive 0x80 (master) no BIOS extensions
3330432 sectors wiped with D2
```

Execute

8. image(src,img.1)

```
            SafeBack 2.0 31Jan00 execution started on Nov 14, 2000 11:21.
11:22:32  Menu selections:
              Function:              Backup
              Remote connection:     Local
              Direct access:         No
              Use XBIOS:             Auto
              Adjust partitions:     No
              Backfill on restore:   Yes
              Compress sector data:  Yes
11:24:37  Backup file F:\F2T15.001 created.
          Backup file comment record:
              Beta3 DI-15 F2->D3->D11  Fill, NO adjust
11:25:18  Backing up drive 0:
          to F:\F2T15.001 on Nov 14, 2000 11:25
11:25:19  Local SafeBack is running on DOS 6.30
          Source drive 0:
              Capacity.......1628 MB
              Cylinders.......827
              Heads..........64
11:25:19  Partition table for drive 0:
11:37:15  Backup file CRC: 82d57464.
11:37:15  Backup of drive 0: completed on Nov 14, 2000 11:37.
          SafeBack execution ended on Nov 14, 2000 11:37.
```

9. baddisk(img,read)

```
return code 00010 on command 00002 from disk 00129 (00254 Max head value)
at address 00438/00127/00040
baddisk  compiled on 11/03/00 at 09:12:12
@(#) Version 1.1 Created 11/03/00 at 09:11:04
return code 00010 on command 00010 from disk 00129 (00254 Max head value)
at address 00438/00127/00040
baddisk  compiled on 11/03/00 at 09:12:12
@(#) Version 1.1 Created 11/03/00 at 09:11:04
```

10. load(img.1,dst)

```
            SafeBack 2.0 31Jan00 execution started on Nov 14, 2000 15:15.
```

```
15:15:57  Menu selections:
             Function:            Restore
             Remote connection:   Local
             Direct access:       No
             Use XBIOS:           Auto
             Adjust partitions:   Auto
             Backfill on restore: Yes
             Compress sector data: Yes
15:16:28  Backup file created on Nov 14, 2000 11:25
          by Gary Fisher Natl Institute of Standards & Technology Software
Diagnostics & Con
          Backup file comment record:
             Beta3 DI-15 F2->D3->D11  Fill, NO adjust
15:16:41  Backup file E:\F2T15.001 opened for access.
15:17:10  Restore of drive 0: from E:\F2T15.001
          to drive 0: started on Nov 14, 2000 15:17
15:17:10  Local SafeBack is running on DOS 6.30
          Source drive 0:
             Capacity.......1628 MB
             Cylinders......827
             Heads..........64
          Destination drive 0:
             Capacity.......1628 MB
             Cylinders......827
             Heads..........64
15:32:53  While reading E:\F2T15.001 at 1402086963, an access denied error
occurred on the backup file.  A
          data block consisting of zeroes was used in place of the data to
          be read.  As a result, another error message will follow this
          one.
15:32:53  F2T15.001, record 2769011 has a CRC error. cc58 was expected, but b38b
read.
15:34:17  Backup file CRC error ignored by recovery at sector 2769011.
15:36:18  Data starting at sector 2769011 and the next 119 sectors is
          questionable due to CRC errors.
15:38:44  CRC mismatch:  Calculated: ca54f2ef, Read: 82d57464
15:45:27  Partition table for drive 0:
15:45:29  Restore of drive 0: to drive 0: completed on Nov 14, 2000 15:45
15:45:37  Menu selections:
             Function:            Restore
             Remote connection:   Local
             Direct access:       No
             Use XBIOS:           Auto
             Adjust partitions:   Auto
             Backfill on restore: Yes
             Compress sector data: Yes
          SafeBack execution ended on Nov 14, 2000 15:45.
```

Measure

11. after=hash(src)

```
A:\DISKHASH.EXE @(#) Version 2.2 Created 10/02/00 at 09:08:26
Comment: beta5 hash F2 after DI-03
run start Sat Nov 18 15:18:39 2000
run finish Sat Nov 18 15:38:57 2000
drive 0x80 (master) no BIOS extensions
Disk SHA-1 hash 96EDE9BC7D9A33A61A5537C5CB7DF45CAD6ED488
```

12. Examine_message(I/O error)

```
15:32:53  F2T15.001, record 2769011 has a CRC error. cc58 was expected, but b38b
read.
```

13. Compare(src,dst)

```
Comment: beta2 DI-24 errors near 686/49/03 (2769041)
run start Tue Nov 14 16:10:52 2000
run finish Tue Nov 14 16:22:27 2000
sectors compared 3330432 match 3330313 differ 119 dropped 0
filled: zero 0 src 0 dst 0 other 0 remainder 0
```

Output Specifications (expected results)

14. before=after

```
before = 96EDE9BC7D9A33A61A5537C5CB7DF45CAD6ED488
after  = 96EDE9BC7D9A33A61A5537C5CB7DF45CAD6ED488
```

15. I/O error message

```
15:32:53  F2T15.001, record 2769011 has a CRC error. cc58 was expected, but b38b
read.
```

16. src and dst compare qualified equal

```
sectors compared 3330432 match 3330313 differ 119 dropped 0
```

Test case ID DI-25

Test assertions

13.   If a duplicate destination partition is created directly from a source partition of the same size, then each sector of the source partition must compare equal to the LBA corresponding sector of the destination partition.

28.   The source before using the tool must be equal to the source after tool use.

Setup

1. wipe(src)

```
A:\DISKWIPE.EXE @(#) Version 2.1 Created 09/27/00 at 13:44:51
Comment: DOS Setup
run start Wed Sep 27 17:47:09 2000
run finish Wed Sep 27 17:54:19 2000
drive 0x80 (master) no BIOS extensions
3330432 sectors wiped with D1
```

2. partition(src,1,*,Fat 12)

3. partition(src,2,*,Small Fat 16)

4. load_os(DOS)

```
Comment: beta5 D1 (DOS) Layout
Source disk partition table
P 000000063 000024129 0000/001/01 0005/063/63 Boot 01 Fat12
X 000024192 003306240 0006/000/01 0825/063/63      05 extended
S 000000063 000044289 0006/001/01 0016/063/63      04 Fat16
x 000044352 003261888 0017/000/01 0825/063/63      05 extended
S 000000063 003261825 0017/001/01 0825/063/63      06 Fat16
Source disk layout:  00826/064/63 3330432 total sectors on disk
      Start LBA   End LBA   Length   Size: MB   (binary)
  0 B         0        62       63    0.03MB    0.03BMB
  1 P        63     24191    24129   12.35MB   11.78BMB
  2 b     24192     24254       63    0.03MB    0.03BMB
  3 P     24255     68543    44289   22.68MB   21.63BMB
  4 b     68544     68606       63    0.03MB    0.03BMB
  5 P     68607   3330431  3261825 1670.05MB 1592.69BMB
```

5. before=hash(src)

```
A:\DISKHASH.EXE @(#) Version 2.1 Created 09/27/00 at 13:44:51
Comment: hash D1 before running SafeBack
run start Fri Sep 29 11:06:09 2000
run finish Fri Sep 29 12:09:44 2000
drive 0x80 (master) no BIOS extensions
Disk SHA-1 hash 305B31403D8AD36BCB9AF108821818DCFA3F919A
```

6. wipe(dst)

```
A:\DISKWIPE.EXE @(#) Version 2.2 Created 10/02/00 at 09:08:26
Comment: Beta4, Wipe D2 (setup for partition copy tests)
run start Mon Oct 23 11:26:16 2000
run finish Mon Oct 23 11:33:38 2000
drive 0x80 (master) no BIOS extensions
3330432 sectors wiped with D2
```

7. partition(dst,1,x,type(src.1)) size(src.1) = x
   Execute

8. copy(src.1,dst.1)

```
          SafeBack 2.0 31Jan00 execution started on Oct 23, 2000 13:27.
13:27:52  Menu selections:
              Function:            Copy
              Remote connection:   Local
              Direct access:       No
              Use XBIOS:           Auto
              Adjust partitions:   Auto
              Backfill on restore: Yes
              Compress sector data: Yes
13:28:53  Copy from Local drive C: to local drive H:
13:29:15  Partition/Boot information saved to A:\PT-DI25.SPS.
13:29:15  Copy of Local drive C: to drive H: begun on Oct 23, 2000 13:29
13:29:15  Local SafeBack is running on DOS 6.30
          Source drive C:
              Capacity........12 MB
              Cylinders.......5
              Heads..........64
          Destination drive H:
              Capacity........12 MB
              Cylinders.......5
              Heads..........64
13:29:20  Copy of drive C: to drive H: completed on Oct 23, 2000 13:29
          SafeBack execution ended on Oct 23, 2000 13:29.
```

   Measure

9. after=hash(src)

```
A:\DISKHASH.EXE @(#) Version 2.2 Created 10/02/00 at 09:08:26
Comment: beta5 Hash of D1 after Tests: DI-25 and DI-39
run start Mon Oct 23 13:55:50 2000
run finish Mon Oct 23 14:17:10 2000
drive 0x80 (master) no BIOS extensions
Disk SHA-1 hash 305B31403D8AD36BCB9AF108821818DCFA3F919A
```

10. Compare(src.1,dst.1)
    Output Specifications (expected results)

11. before=after

```
before = 305B31403D8AD36BCB9AF108821818DCFA3F919A
after  = 305B31403D8AD36BCB9AF108821818DCFA3F919A
```

12. src and dst compare equal

```
sectors compared 24129 match 24129 differ 0 dropped 0
```

Test case ID DI-32

Test assertions

_14._   _If a duplicate destination partition is created directly from a smaller source partition, then each sector of the source partition must compare equal to the LBA corresponding sector of the destination partition._

_15._   _If a duplicate destination partition is created directly from a smaller source partition, then each sector of the destination partition with no LBA corresponding sector in the source partition must be as specified by the tool (if the tool allows such a specification). Otherwise each bit of each sector must be set to zero._

_28._   _The source before using the tool must be equal to the source after tool use._

_29._   _The results of any remote tool use must be equal to the results of local identical tool use._

  Setup

1. wipe(src)

```
A:\DISKWIPE.EXE @(#) Version 2.1 Created 09/27/00 at 13:44:51
Comment: DOS Setup
run start Wed Sep 27 17:47:09 2000
run finish Wed Sep 27 17:54:19 2000
drive 0x80 (master) no BIOS extensions
3330432 sectors wiped with D1
```

2. partition(src,1,*,Small Fat 16)

3. partition(src,2,*,Fat 12)

4. load_os(DOS)

```
Comment: beta5 D1 (DOS) Layout
Source disk partition table
P 000000063 000024129 0000/001/01 0005/063/63 Boot 01 Fat12
X 000024192 003306240 0006/000/01 0825/063/63      05 extended
S 000000063 000044289 0006/001/01 0016/063/63      04 Fat16
x 000044352 003261888 0017/000/01 0825/063/63      05 extended
S 000000063 003261825 0017/001/01 0825/063/63      06 Fat16
Source disk layout:  00826/064/63 3330432 total sectors on disk
      Start LBA   End LBA    Length    Size: MB   (binary)
  0 B         0        62        63     0.03MB     0.03BMB
  1 P        63     24191     24129    12.35MB    11.78BMB
  2 b     24192     24254        63     0.03MB     0.03BMB
  3 P     24255     68543     44289    22.68MB    21.63BMB
  4 b     68544     68606        63     0.03MB     0.03BMB
  5 P     68607   3330431   3261825  1670.05MB  1592.69BMB
```

5. before=hash(src)

```
A:\DISKHASH.EXE @(#) Version 2.1 Created 09/27/00 at 13:44:51
Comment: hash D1 before running SafeBack
run start Fri Sep 29 11:06:09 2000
run finish Fri Sep 29 12:09:44 2000
drive 0x80 (master) no BIOS extensions
Disk SHA-1 hash 305B31403D8AD36BCB9AF108821818DCFA3F919A
```

6. wipe(dst)

```
A:\DISKWIPE.EXE @(#) Version 2.2 Created 10/02/00 at 09:08:26
Comment: Beta4, Wipe D2 (setup for partition copy tests)
run start Mon Oct 23 11:26:16 2000
run finish Mon Oct 23 11:33:38 2000
drive 0x80 (master) no BIOS extensions
3330432 sectors wiped with D2
```

7. partition(dst,1,x,type(src.1)) size(src.1) < x
   Execute
8. establish_link()
9. copy(src.1,dst.1,n)

```
            SafeBack 2.0 31Jan00 execution started on Oct 23, 2000 15:52.
15:53:02  Menu selections:
            Function:              Copy
            Remote connection:     LPT1:
            Direct access:         No
            Use XBIOS:             Auto
            Adjust partitions:     Auto
            Backfill on restore:   No
            Compress sector data:  Yes
15:58:13  Copy from Remote drive D: to local drive K:
15:58:31  Partition/Boot information saved to A:\PT-DI-32.SPS.
15:58:32  Copy of Remote drive D: to drive K: begun on Oct 23, 2000 15:58
15:58:32  Local SafeBack is running on DOS 6.30
15:58:32  Remote SafeBack server is running on DOS 6.30
            Source drive D:
                Capacity........22 MB
                Cylinders.......10
                Heads...........64
            Destination drive K:
                Capacity........26 MB
                Cylinders.......12
                Heads...........64
16:04:57  Copy of drive D: to drive K: completed on Oct 23, 2000 16:04
            SafeBack execution ended on Oct 23, 2000 16:05.
```

   Measure
10. after=hash(src)
```
A:\DISKHASH.EXE @(#) Version 2.2 Created 10/02/00 at 09:08:26
Comment: beta5 hash D1 after DI-32
run start Mon Oct 23 16:20:32 2000
run finish Mon Oct 23 16:41:06 2000
drive 0x80 (master) no BIOS extensions
Disk SHA-1 hash 305B31403D8AD36BCB9AF108821818DCFA3F919A
```
11. Compare(src.1,dst.1)

   Output Specifications (expected results)
12. before=after
```
before = 305B31403D8AD36BCB9AF108821818DCFA3F919A
after  = 305B31403D8AD36BCB9AF108821818DCFA3F919A
```
13. src and dst compare equal
```
sectors compared 44289 match 44289 differ 0 dropped 0
```

Test case ID DI-33

Test assertions

14.   If a duplicate destination partition is created directly from a smaller source partition, then each sector of the source partition must compare equal to the LBA corresponding sector of the destination partition.

15.   If a duplicate destination partition is created directly from a smaller source partition, then each sector of the destination partition with no LBA corresponding sector in the source partition must be as specified by the tool (if the tool allows such a specification). Otherwise each bit of each sector must be set to zero.

28. *The source before using the tool must be equal to the source after tool use.*
  Setup

1. wipe(src)
```
A:\DISKWIPE.EXE @(#) Version 2.1 Created 09/27/00 at 13:44:51
Comment: Windows 95 setup
run start Wed Sep 27 17:52:35 2000
run finish Wed Sep 27 17:59:47 2000
drive 0x80 (master) no BIOS extensions
3330432 sectors wiped with F1
```
2. partition(src,1,*,Big Fat 16)
3. load_os(Windows 95)
```
Comment: beta5 F1 W95 layout
Source disk partition table
P 000000063 003072321 0000/001/01 0761/063/63 Boot 06 Fat16
X 003072384 000258048 0762/000/01 0825/063/63      05 extended
S 000000063 000104769 0762/001/01 0787/063/63      06 Fat16
x 000104832 000153216 0788/000/01 0825/063/63      05 extended
S 000000063 000153153 0788/001/01 0825/063/63      06 Fat16
Source disk layout:  00826/064/63 3330432 total sectors on disk
      Start LBA    End LBA    Length    Size: MB   (binary)
  0 B         0        62        63     0.03MB     0.03BMB
  1 P        63   3072383   3072321  1573.03MB  1500.16BMB
  2 b   3072384   3072446        63     0.03MB     0.03BMB
  3 P   3072447   3177215    104769    53.64MB    51.16BMB
  4 b   3177216   3177278        63     0.03MB     0.03BMB
  5 P   3177279   3330431    153153    78.41MB    74.78BMB
```
4. before=hash(src)
```
A:\DISKHASH.EXE @(#) Version 2.2 Created 10/02/00 at 09:08:26
Comment: rehash F1 (Win 95)
run start Fri Nov 03 14:08:19 2000
run finish Fri Nov 03 14:28:46 2000
drive 0x80 (master) no BIOS extensions
Disk SHA-1 hash 5FBEEB219E7282ED621645A67252A70F4D8BBF21
```
5. wipe(dst)
```
A:\DISKWIPE.EXE @(#) Version 2.2 Created 10/02/00 at 09:08:26
Comment: Beta5 DI-33,40,54,61 (partition operations)
run start Tue Nov 28 11:57:54 2000
run finish Tue Nov 28 12:05:34 2000
drive 0x80 (master) no BIOS extensions
3330432 sectors wiped with D2
```
6. partition(dst,1,x,type(src.1)) size(src.1) < x
  Execute

7. copy(src.1,dst.1,n)
```
          SafeBack 2.0 31Jan00 execution started on Nov 28, 2000 14:39.
14:39:24  Menu selections:
             Function:              Copy
             Remote connection:     Local
             Direct access:         No
             Use XBIOS:             Auto
             Adjust partitions:     Auto
             Backfill on restore:   No
             Compress sector data:  Yes
14:39:59  Copy from Local drive E: to local drive G:
14:40:08  Partition/Boot information saved to A:\PT-DI-33.SPS.
14:40:08  Copy of Local drive E: to drive G: begun on Nov 28, 2000 14:40
```

```
14:40:08   Local SafeBack is running on DOS 6.30
           Source drive E:
              Capacity........51 MB
              Cylinders.......25
              Heads..........64
           Destination drive G:
              Capacity........67 MB
              Cylinders.......33
              Heads..........64
14:40:35   Copy of drive E: to drive G: completed on Nov 28, 2000 14:40
           SafeBack execution ended on Nov 28, 2000 14:40.
```
   Measure

8. after=hash(src)
```
A:\DISKHASH.EXE %Z% Version %I% Created %G% at %U%
Comment: beta5 hash F1 after DI-02,14,33,40,54,61
run start Tue Nov 28 15:03:27 2000
run finish Tue Nov 28 15:24:20 2000
drive 0x80 (master) no BIOS extensions
Disk SHA-1 hash 5FBEEB219E7282ED621645A67252A70F4D8BBF21
```
9. Compare(src.1,dst.1)

   Output Specifications (expected results)

10. before=after
```
before = 5FBEEB219E7282ED621645A67252A70F4D8BBF21
after  = 5FBEEB219E7282ED621645A67252A70F4D8BBF21
```
11. src and dst compare equal
```
sectors compared 104769 match 104769 differ 0 dropped 0
```

Test case ID DI-39

Test assertions

16.   If a duplicate destination partition is created directly from a larger source partition, then each sector of the destination partition must compare equal to the LBA corresponding sector of the source partition.

17.   If a duplicate destination partition is created directly from a larger source partition, then the tool must notify the user.

28.   The source before using the tool must be equal to the source after tool use.

   Setup

1. wipe(src)
```
A:\DISKWIPE.EXE @(#) Version 2.1 Created 09/27/00 at 13:44:51
Comment: DOS Setup
run start Wed Sep 27 17:47:09 2000
run finish Wed Sep 27 17:54:19 2000
drive 0x80 (master) no BIOS extensions
3330432 sectors wiped with D1
```
2. partition(src,1,*,Small Fat 16)

3. partition(src,2,*,Fat 12)

4. load_os(DOS)
```
Comment: beta5 D1 (DOS) Layout
Source disk partition table
P 000000063 000024129 0000/001/01 0005/063/63 Boot 01 Fat12
X 000024192 003306240 0006/000/01 0825/063/63      05 extended
S 000000063 000044289 0006/001/01 0016/063/63      04 Fat16
x 000044352 003261888 0017/000/01 0825/063/63      05 extended
```

70

```
S 000000063 003261825 0017/001/01 0825/063/63     06 Fat16
Source disk layout:  00826/064/63 3330432 total sectors on disk
       Start LBA   End LBA    Length    Size: MB   (binary)
  0 B         0        62        63     0.03MB     0.03BMB
  1 P        63     24191     24129    12.35MB    11.78BMB
  2 b     24192     24254        63     0.03MB     0.03BMB
  3 P     24255     68543     44289    22.68MB    21.63BMB
  4 b     68544     68606        63     0.03MB     0.03BMB
  5 P     68607   3330431   3261825  1670.05MB  1592.69BMB
```

5. before=hash(src)

```
A:\DISKHASH.EXE @(#) Version 2.1 Created 09/27/00 at 13:44:51
Comment: hash D1 before running SafeBack
run start Fri Sep 29 11:06:09 2000
run finish Fri Sep 29 12:09:44 2000
drive 0x80 (master) no BIOS extensions
Disk SHA-1 hash 305B31403D8AD36BCB9AF108821818DCFA3F919A
```

6. wipe(dst)

```
A:\DISKWIPE.EXE @(#) Version 2.2 Created 10/02/00 at 09:08:26
Comment: Beta4, Wipe D2 (setup for partition copy tests)
run start Mon Oct 23 11:26:16 2000
run finish Mon Oct 23 11:33:38 2000
drive 0x80 (master) no BIOS extensions
3330432 sectors wiped with D2
```

7. partition(dst,1,x,type(src.1)) size(src.1) > x
   Execute

8. copy(src.1,dst.1)

```
           SafeBack 2.0 31Jan00 execution started on Oct 23, 2000 13:41.
13:42:03   Menu selections:
               Function:              Copy
               Remote connection:     Local
               Direct access:         No
               Use XBIOS:             Auto
               Adjust partitions:     Auto
               Backfill on restore:   Yes
               Compress sector data:  Yes
13:48:08   Menu selections:
               Function:              Copy
               Remote connection:     Local
               Direct access:         No
               Use XBIOS:             Auto
               Adjust partitions:     Auto
               Backfill on restore:   Yes
               Compress sector data:  Yes
13:49:55   Copy from Local drive E: to local drive J:
13:49:55   Insufficient destination file space projected.
13:50:23   Partition/Boot information saved to A:\PT-DI39.SPS.
13:50:23   Copy of Local drive E: to drive J: begun on Oct 23, 2000 13:50
13:50:23   Local SafeBack is running on DOS 6.30
           Source drive E:
               Capacity........22 MB
               Cylinders.......10
               Heads...........64
           Destination drive J:
               Capacity........20 MB
               Cylinders.......9
               Heads...........64
```

```
13:50:30  Copy of drive E: to drive J: completed on Oct 23, 2000 13:50
          SafeBack execution ended on Oct 23, 2000 13:51.
```
Measure
9. after=hash(src)
```
A:\DISKHASH.EXE @(#) Version 2.2 Created 10/02/00 at 09:08:26
Comment: beta5 Hash of D1 after Tests: DI-25 and DI-39
run start Mon Oct 23 13:55:50 2000
run finish Mon Oct 23 14:17:10 2000
drive 0x80 (master) no BIOS extensions
Disk SHA-1 hash 305B31403D8AD36BCB9AF108821818DCFA3F919A
```
10. Examine_message(Destination too small)
```
13:49:55  Insufficient destination file space projected.
```
11. Compare(src.1,dst.1)
   Output Specifications (expected results)
12. before=after
```
before = 305B31403D8AD36BCB9AF108821818DCFA3F919A
after  = 305B31403D8AD36BCB9AF108821818DCFA3F919A
```
13. Destination too small message
```
13:49:55  Insufficient destination file space projected.
```
14. src and dst compare equal
```
sectors compared 40257 match 40257 differ 0 dropped 4032
```

Test case ID DI-40

Test assertions
16.   If a duplicate destination partition is created directly from a larger source partition, then each sector of the destination partition must compare equal to the LBA corresponding sector of the source partition.
17.   If a duplicate destination partition is created directly from a larger source partition, then the tool must notify the user.
28.   The source before using the tool must be equal to the source after tool use.
   Setup
1. wipe(src)
```
A:\DISKWIPE.EXE @(#) Version 2.1 Created 09/27/00 at 13:44:51
Comment: Windows 95 setup
run start Wed Sep 27 17:52:35 2000
run finish Wed Sep 27 17:59:47 2000
drive 0x80 (master) no BIOS extensions
3330432 sectors wiped with F1
```
2. partition(src,1,*,Big Fat 16)
3. load_os(Windows 95)
```
Comment: beta5 F1 W95 layout
Source disk partition table
P 000000063 003072321 0000/001/01 0761/063/63 Boot 06 Fat16
X 003072384 000258048 0762/000/01 0825/063/63      05 extended
S 000000063 000104769 0762/001/01 0787/063/63      06 Fat16
x 000104832 000153216 0788/000/01 0825/063/63      05 extended
S 000000063 000153153 0788/001/01 0825/063/63      06 Fat16
Source disk layout:   00826/064/63 3330432 total sectors on disk
     Start LBA    End LBA    Length    Size: MB    (binary)
  0 B        0         62        63     0.03MB      0.03BMB
  1 P       63    3072383   3072321  1573.03MB   1500.16BMB
  2 b  3072384    3072446        63     0.03MB      0.03BMB
  3 P  3072447    3177215    104769    53.64MB     51.16BMB
```

```
  4 b    3177216    3177278        63     0.03MB     0.03BMB
  5 P    3177279    3330431    153153    78.41MB    74.78BMB
```

4. before=hash(src)

```
A:\DISKHASH.EXE @(#) Version 2.2 Created 10/02/00 at 09:08:26
Comment: rehash F1 (Win 95)
run start Fri Nov 03 14:08:19 2000
run finish Fri Nov 03 14:28:46 2000
drive 0x80 (master) no BIOS extensions
Disk SHA-1 hash 5FBEEB219E7282ED621645A67252A70F4D8BBF21
```

5. wipe(dst)

```
A:\DISKWIPE.EXE @(#) Version 2.2 Created 10/02/00 at 09:08:26
Comment: Beta5 DI-33,40,54,61 (partition operations)
run start Tue Nov 28 11:57:54 2000
run finish Tue Nov 28 12:05:34 2000
drive 0x80 (master) no BIOS extensions
3330432 sectors wiped with D2
```

6. partition(dst,1,x,type(src.1)) size(src.1) > x

Execute

7. copy(src.1,dst.1)

```
            SafeBack 2.0 31Jan00 execution started on Nov 28, 2000 14:41.
14:41:41  Menu selections:
              Function:            Copy
              Remote connection:   Local
              Direct access:       No
              Use XBIOS:           Auto
              Adjust partitions:   Auto
              Backfill on restore: Yes
              Compress sector data: Yes
14:42:02  Copy from Local drive E: to local drive H:
14:42:02  Insufficient destination file space projected.
14:42:15  Partition/Boot information saved to A:\PT-DI-40.SPS.
14:42:16  Copy of Local drive E: to drive H: begun on Nov 28, 2000 14:42
14:42:16  Local SafeBack is running on DOS 6.30
          Source drive E:
              Capacity........51 MB
              Cylinders.......25
              Heads...........64
          Destination drive H:
              Capacity........45 MB
              Cylinders.......22
              Heads...........64
14:42:39  Copy of drive E: to drive H: completed on Nov 28, 2000 14:42
          SafeBack execution ended on Nov 28, 2000 14:42.
```

Measure

8. after=hash(src)

```
A:\DISKHASH.EXE %Z% Version %I% Created %G% at %U%
Comment: beta5 hash F1 after DI-02,14,33,40,54,61
run start Tue Nov 28 15:03:27 2000
run finish Tue Nov 28 15:24:20 2000
drive 0x80 (master) no BIOS extensions
Disk SHA-1 hash 5FBEEB219E7282ED621645A67252A70F4D8BBF21
```

9. Examine_message(Destination too small)

```
14:42:02  Insufficient destination file space projected.
```

10. Compare(src.1,dst.1)

Output Specifications (expected results)

11. before=after

```
before = 5FBEEB219E7282ED621645A67252A70F4D8BBF21
after  = 5FBEEB219E7282ED621645A67252A70F4D8BBF21
```

12. Destination too small message

```
14:42:02  Insufficient destination file space projected.
```

13. src and dst compare equal

```
sectors compared 92673 match 92673 differ 0 dropped 12096
```

Test case ID DI-46

Test assertions

18.   If a duplicate destination partition is created from an image file of a source partition of the same size, then each sector of the source partition must compare equal to the LBA corresponding sector of the destination partition.

28.   The source before using the tool must be equal to the source after tool use.

Setup

1. wipe(src)

```
A:\DISKWIPE.EXE @(#) Version 2.1 Created 09/27/00 at 13:44:51
Comment: DOS Setup
run start Wed Sep 27 17:47:09 2000
run finish Wed Sep 27 17:54:19 2000
drive 0x80 (master) no BIOS extensions
3330432 sectors wiped with D1
```

2. partition(src,1,*,Small Fat 16)
3. partition(src,2,*,Fat 12)
4. load_os(DOS)

```
Comment: beta5 D1 (DOS) Layout
Source disk partition table
P 000000063 000024129 0000/001/01 0005/063/63 Boot 01 Fat12
X 000024192 003306240 0006/000/01 0825/063/63     05 extended
S 000000063 000044289 0006/001/01 0016/063/63     04 Fat16
x 000044352 003261888 0017/000/01 0825/063/63     05 extended
S 000000063 003261825 0017/001/01 0825/063/63     06 Fat16
Source disk layout:  00826/064/63 3330432 total sectors on disk
     Start LBA    End LBA    Length    Size: MB    (binary)
 0 B         0         62        63     0.03MB    0.03BMB
 1 P        63      24191     24129    12.35MB   11.78BMB
 2 b     24192      24254        63     0.03MB    0.03BMB
 3 P     24255      68543     44289    22.68MB   21.63BMB
 4 b     68544      68606        63     0.03MB    0.03BMB
 5 P     68607    3330431   3261825  1670.05MB 1592.69BMB
```

5. before=hash(src)

```
A:\DISKHASH.EXE @(#) Version 2.1 Created 09/27/00 at 13:44:51
Comment: hash D1 before running SafeBack
run start Fri Sep 29 11:06:09 2000
run finish Fri Sep 29 12:09:44 2000
drive 0x80 (master) no BIOS extensions
Disk SHA-1 hash 305B31403D8AD36BCB9AF108821818DCFA3F919A
```

6. wipe(img)
7. partition(img,1,MAX,Big Fat 16)
8. wipe(dst)

```
A:\DISKWIPE.EXE @(#) Version 2.2 Created 10/02/00 at 09:08:26
```

```
Comment: Beta4, Wipe D2 (setup for partition copy tests)
run start Mon Oct 23 11:26:16 2000
run finish Mon Oct 23 11:33:38 2000
drive 0x80 (master) no BIOS extensions
3330432 sectors wiped with D2
```

9. partition(dst,1,x,type(src.1)) size(src.1) = x
    Execute

10. image(src.1,img.1)

```
                SafeBack 2.0 31Jan00 execution started on Oct 24, 2000 14:10.
14:10:41  Menu selections:
                Function:           Backup
                Remote connection:  Local
                Direct access:      No
                Use XBIOS:          Auto
                Adjust partitions:  Auto
                Backfill on restore: Yes
                Compress sector data: Yes
14:11:56  Menu selections:
                Function:           Backup
                Remote connection:  Local
                Direct access:      No
                Use XBIOS:          Auto
                Adjust partitions:  Auto
                Backfill on restore: Yes
                Compress sector data: Yes
14:12:22  Backup file D:\DI-46.001 created.
          Backup file comment record:
                DI-46 D1==>D2
14:12:40  Backing up drive E:
          to D:\DI-46.001 on Oct 24, 2000 14:12
14:12:40  Local SafeBack is running on DOS 6.30
          Source drive E:
              Capacity........22 MB
              Cylinders.......10
              Heads...........64
14:12:55  Backup file CRC: 9829a14b.
14:12:55  Backup of drive E: completed on Oct 24, 2000 14:12.
          SafeBack execution ended on Oct 24, 2000 14:13.
```

11. load(img.1,dst.1)

```
                SafeBack 2.0 31Jan00 execution started on Oct 24, 2000 14:14.
14:14:16  Menu selections:
                Function:           Restore
                Remote connection:  Local
                Direct access:      No
                Use XBIOS:          Auto
                Adjust partitions:  Auto
                Backfill on restore: Yes
                Compress sector data: Yes
14:14:29  Backup file created on Oct 24, 2000 14:12
          by Gary Fisher Natl Institute of Standards & Technology Software
Diagnostics & Con
          Backup file comment record:
                DI-46 D1==>D2
14:14:35  Backup file D:\DI-46.001 opened for access.
14:15:03  Partition/Boot information saved to A:\PT-DI-46.SPS.
14:15:03  Restore of drive E: from D:\DI-46.001
          to drive J: started on Oct 24, 2000 14:15
```

```
14:15:03   Local SafeBack is running on DOS 6.30
           Source drive E:
              Capacity........22 MB
              Cylinders.......10
              Heads...........64
           Destination drive J:
              Capacity........22 MB
              Cylinders.......10
              Heads...........64
14:15:36   The whole-file CRC verifies:  9829a14b
14:15:36   Restore of drive E: to drive J: completed on Oct 24, 2000 14:15
14:15:43   Menu selections:
              Function:             Restore
              Remote connection:    Local
              Direct access:        No
              Use XBIOS:            Auto
              Adjust partitions:    Auto
              Backfill on restore:  Yes
              Compress sector data: Yes
           SafeBack execution ended on Oct 24, 2000 14:15.
```

   Measure

12. after=hash(src)

```
A:\DISKHASH.EXE @(#) Version 2.2 Created 10/02/00 at 09:08:26
Comment: beta5 hash disk after DI-21
run start Mon Nov 20 11:41:49 2000
run finish Mon Nov 20 12:02:03 2000
drive 0x80 (master) no BIOS extensions
Disk SHA-1 hash 305B31403D8AD36BCB9AF108821818DCFA3F919A
```

13. Compare(src.1,dst.1)

   Output Specifications (expected results)

14. before=after

```
before = 305B31403D8AD36BCB9AF108821818DCFA3F919A
after  = 305B31403D8AD36BCB9AF108821818DCFA3F919A
```

15. src and dst compare equal

```
sectors compared 44289 match 44289 differ 0 dropped 0
```

Test case ID DI-53

Test assertions

19.   *If a duplicate destination partition is created from an image file of a smaller source partition, then each sector of the source partition must compare equal to the LBA corresponding sector of the destination partition.*

20.   *If a duplicate destination partition is created from an image file of a smaller source partition, then each sector of the destination partition with no LBA corresponding sector in the source partition must be as specified by the tool (if the tool allows such a specification). Otherwise each bit of each sector must be set to zero.*

28.   *The source before using the tool must be equal to the source after tool use.*

29.   *The results of any remote tool use must be equal to the results of local identical tool use.*

   Setup

1. wipe(src)

```
A:\DISKWIPE.EXE @(#) Version 2.1 Created 09/27/00 at 13:44:51
Comment: DOS Setup
run start Wed Sep 27 17:47:09 2000
run finish Wed Sep 27 17:54:19 2000
```

```
drive 0x80 (master) no BIOS extensions
3330432 sectors wiped with D1
```

2. partition(src,1,*,Fat 12)
3. partition(src,2,*,Small Fat 16)
4. load_os(DOS)

```
Comment: beta5 D1 (DOS) Layout
Source disk partition table
P 000000063 000024129 0000/001/01 0005/063/63 Boot 01 Fat12
X 000024192 003306240 0006/000/01 0825/063/63      05 extended
S 000000063 000044289 0006/001/01 0016/063/63      04 Fat16
x 000044352 003261888 0017/000/01 0825/063/63      05 extended
S 000000063 003261825 0017/001/01 0825/063/63      06 Fat16
Source disk layout:  00826/064/63 3330432 total sectors on disk
      Start LBA   End LBA   Length   Size: MB   (binary)
  0 B         0        62       63    0.03MB    0.03BMB
  1 P        63     24191    24129   12.35MB   11.78BMB
  2 b     24192     24254       63    0.03MB    0.03BMB
  3 P     24255     68543    44289   22.68MB   21.63BMB
  4 b     68544     68606       63    0.03MB    0.03BMB
  5 P     68607   3330431  3261825 1670.05MB 1592.69BMB
```

5. before=hash(src)

```
A:\DISKHASH.EXE @(#) Version 2.1 Created 09/27/00 at 13:44:51
Comment: hash D1 before running SafeBack
run start Fri Sep 29 11:06:09 2000
run finish Fri Sep 29 12:09:44 2000
drive 0x80 (master) no BIOS extensions
Disk SHA-1 hash 305B31403D8AD36BCB9AF108821818DCFA3F919A
```

6. wipe(img)
7. partition(img,1,MAX,Big Fat 16)
8. wipe(dst)

```
A:\DISKWIPE.EXE @(#) Version 2.2 Created 10/02/00 at 09:08:26
Comment: Beta4, Wipe D2 (setup for partition copy tests)
run start Mon Oct 23 11:26:16 2000
run finish Mon Oct 23 11:33:38 2000
drive 0x80 (master) no BIOS extensions
3330432 sectors wiped with D2
```

9. partition(dst,1,x,type(src.1)) size(src.1) < x
    Execute

10. establish_link()
11. image(src.1,img.1,f)

```
          SafeBack 2.0 31Jan00 execution started on Oct 24, 2000 15:30.
15:30:22  Menu selections:
          Function:             Backup
          Remote connection:    Local
          Direct access:        No
          Use XBIOS:            Auto
          Adjust partitions:    Auto
          Backfill on restore:  Yes
          Compress sector data: Yes
15:30:42  Menu selections:
          Function:             Backup
          Remote connection:    LPT1:
          Direct access:        No
          Use XBIOS:            Auto
          Adjust partitions:    Auto
```

```
              Backfill on restore:     Yes
              Compress sector data:    Yes
15:32:20   Backup file C:\DI-53.001 created.
           Backup file comment record:
             DI-53 beta3:D1==>beta4:D2
15:33:05   Backing up drive C:
           to C:\DI-53.001 on Oct 24, 2000 15:33
15:33:05   Local SafeBack is running on DOS 6.30
15:33:05   Remote SafeBack server is running on DOS 6.30
           Source drive C:
              Capacity........12 MB
              Cylinders.......5
              Heads...........64
15:36:36   Backup file CRC: 3f3fa343.
15:36:36   Backup of drive C: completed on Oct 24, 2000 15:36.
           SafeBack execution ended on Oct 24, 2000 15:38.
```

12. load(img.1,dst.1)

```
           SafeBack 2.0 31Jan00 execution started on Oct 24, 2000 15:47.
15:47:44   Menu selections:
              Function:               Restore
              Remote connection:      Local
              Direct access:          No
              Use XBIOS:              Auto
              Adjust partitions:      Auto
              Backfill on restore:    Yes
              Compress sector data:   Yes
15:48:04   Backup file created on Oct 24, 2000 15:33
           by Gary Fisher Natl Institute of Standards & Technology Software
Diagnostics & Con
           Backup file comment record:
             DI-53 beta3:D1==>beta4:D2
15:48:07   Backup file D:\DI-53.001 opened for access.
15:48:46   Partition/Boot information saved to A:\PT-DI-53.SPS.
15:48:47   Restore of drive C: from D:\DI-53.001
           to drive I: started on Oct 24, 2000 15:48
15:48:47   Local SafeBack is running on DOS 6.30
           Source drive C:
              Capacity........12 MB
              Cylinders.......5
              Heads...........64
           Destination drive I:
              Capacity........14 MB
              Cylinders.......6
              Heads...........64
15:49:05   The whole-file CRC verifies:  3f3fa343
15:49:10   Restore of drive C: to drive I: completed on Oct 24, 2000 15:49
15:49:20   Menu selections:
              Function:               Restore
              Remote connection:      Local
              Direct access:          No
              Use XBIOS:              Auto
              Adjust partitions:      Auto
              Backfill on restore:    Yes
              Compress sector data:   Yes
           SafeBack execution ended on Oct 24, 2000 15:49.
```

Measure

13. after=hash(src)
```
A:\DISKHASH.EXE @(#) Version 2.2 Created 10/02/00 at 09:08:26
Comment: beta5 hash disk after DI-21
run start Mon Nov 20 11:41:49 2000
run finish Mon Nov 20 12:02:03 2000
drive 0x80 (master) no BIOS extensions
Disk SHA-1 hash 305B31403D8AD36BCB9AF108821818DCFA3F919A
```
14. Compare(src.1,dst.1)

  Output Specifications (expected results)

15. before=after
```
before = 305B31403D8AD36BCB9AF108821818DCFA3F919A
after  = 305B31403D8AD36BCB9AF108821818DCFA3F919A
```
16. src and dst compare equal
```
sectors compared 24129 match 24129 differ 0 dropped 0
```

Test case ID DI-54

Test assertions

19.   If a duplicate destination partition is created from an image file of a smaller source partition, then each sector of the source partition must compare equal to the LBA corresponding sector of the destination partition.

20.   If a duplicate destination partition is created from an image file of a smaller source partition, then each sector of the destination partition with no LBA corresponding sector in the source partition must be as specified by the tool (if the tool allows such a specification). Otherwise each bit of each sector must be set to zero.

28.   The source before using the tool must be equal to the source after tool use.

  Setup

1. wipe(src)
```
A:\DISKWIPE.EXE @(#) Version 2.1 Created 09/27/00 at 13:44:51
Comment: Windows 95 setup
run start Wed Sep 27 17:52:35 2000
run finish Wed Sep 27 17:59:47 2000
drive 0x80 (master) no BIOS extensions
3330432 sectors wiped with F1
```
2. partition(src,1,*,Big Fat 16)

3. load_os(Windows 95)
```
Comment: beta5 F1 W95 layout
Source disk partition table
P 000000063 003072321 0000/001/01 0761/063/63 Boot 06 Fat16
X 003072384 000258048 0762/000/01 0825/063/63      05 extended
S 000000063 000104769 0762/001/01 0787/063/63      06 Fat16
x 000104832 000153216 0788/000/01 0825/063/63      05 extended
S 000000063 000153153 0788/001/01 0825/063/63      06 Fat16
Source disk layout: 00826/064/63 3330432 total sectors on disk
      Start LBA   End LBA    Length    Size: MB    (binary)
  0 B         0        62        63     0.03MB     0.03BMB
  1 P        63   3072383   3072321  1573.03MB  1500.16BMB
  2 b   3072384   3072446        63     0.03MB     0.03BMB
  3 P   3072447   3177215    104769    53.64MB    51.16BMB
  4 b   3177216   3177278        63     0.03MB     0.03BMB
  5 P   3177279   3330431    153153    78.41MB    74.78BMB
```
4. before=hash(src)
```
A:\DISKHASH.EXE @(#) Version 2.2 Created 10/02/00 at 09:08:26
Comment: rehash F1 (Win 95)
```

79

```
run start Fri Nov 03 14:08:19 2000
run finish Fri Nov 03 14:28:46 2000
drive 0x80 (master) no BIOS extensions
Disk SHA-1 hash 5FBEEB219E7282ED621645A67252A70F4D8BBF21
```
5. wipe(img)
6. partition(img,1,MAX,Big Fat 16)
7. wipe(dst)
```
A:\DISKWIPE.EXE @(#) Version 2.2 Created 10/02/00 at 09:08:26
Comment: Beta5 DI-33,40,54,61 (partition operations)
run start Tue Nov 28 11:57:54 2000
run finish Tue Nov 28 12:05:34 2000
drive 0x80 (master) no BIOS extensions
3330432 sectors wiped with D2
```
8. partition(dst,1,x,type(src.1)) size(src.1) < x
   Execute
9. image(src.1,img.1,f)
```
          SafeBack 2.0 31Jan00 execution started on Nov 28, 2000 14:22.
14:23:14  Menu selections:
              Function:            Backup
              Remote connection:   Local
              Direct access:       No
              Use XBIOS:           Auto
              Adjust partitions:   Auto
              Backfill on restore: Yes
              Compress sector data: Yes
14:25:11  Backup file I:\F1I54.001 created.
          Backup file comment record:
              beta2 backup F1->D3->D2
14:25:35  Backing up drive E:
          to I:\F1I54.001 on Nov 28, 2000 14:25
14:25:37  Local SafeBack is running on DOS 6.30
          Source drive E:
              Capacity........51 MB
              Cylinders.......25
              Heads...........64
14:26:07  Backup file CRC: b2a7c181.
14:26:07  Backup of drive E: completed on Nov 28, 2000 14:26.
          SafeBack execution ended on Nov 28, 2000 14:26.
```
10. load(img.1,dst.1)
```
          SafeBack 2.0 31Jan00 execution started on Nov 28, 2000 14:32.
14:32:55  Menu selections:
              Function:            Restore
              Remote connection:   Local
              Direct access:       No
              Use XBIOS:           Auto
              Adjust partitions:   Auto
              Backfill on restore: Yes
              Compress sector data: Yes
14:33:08  Backup file created on Nov 28, 2000 14:25
          by Gary Fisher Natl Institute of Standards & Technology Software
Diagnostics & Con
          Backup file comment record:
              beta2 backup F1->D3->D2
14:33:13  Backup file K:\F1I54.001 opened for access.
14:33:38  Partition/Boot information saved to A:\PT-DI-54.SPS.
```

```
14:33:39   Restore of drive E: from K:\F1I54.001
           to drive G: started on Nov 28, 2000 14:33
14:33:39   Local SafeBack is running on DOS 6.30
           Source drive E:
              Capacity........51 MB
              Cylinders.......25
              Heads..........64
           Destination drive G:
              Capacity........71 MB
              Cylinders.......35
              Heads..........64
14:34:10   The whole-file CRC verifies:  b2a7c181
14:34:13   Restore of drive E: to drive G: completed on Nov 28, 2000 14:34
14:34:20   Menu selections:
              Function:             Restore
              Remote connection:    Local
              Direct access:        No
              Use XBIOS:            Auto
              Adjust partitions:    Auto
              Backfill on restore:  Yes
              Compress sector data: Yes
           SafeBack execution ended on Nov 28, 2000 14:34.
```

   Measure

11. after=hash(src)

```
A:\DISKHASH.EXE %Z% Version %I% Created %G% at %U%
Comment: beta5 hash F1 after DI-02,14,33,40,54,61
run start Tue Nov 28 15:03:27 2000
run finish Tue Nov 28 15:24:20 2000
drive 0x80 (master) no BIOS extensions
Disk SHA-1 hash 5FBEEB219E7282ED621645A67252A70F4D8BBF21
```

12. Compare(src.1,dst.1)

   Output Specifications (expected results)

13. before=after

```
before = 5FBEEB219E7282ED621645A67252A70F4D8BBF21
after  = 5FBEEB219E7282ED621645A67252A70F4D8BBF21
```

14. src and dst compare equal

```
sectors compared 104769 match 104769 differ 0 dropped 0
```

Test case ID DI-60

Test assertions

21.   If a duplicate destination partition is created from an image file of a larger source partition, then each sector of the destination partition must compare equal to the LBA corresponding sector of the source partition.

22.   If a duplicate destination partition is created from an image file of a larger source partition, then the tool must notify the user.

28.   The source before using the tool must be equal to the source after tool use.

   Setup

1. wipe(src)

```
A:\DISKWIPE.EXE @(#) Version 2.1 Created 09/27/00 at 13:44:51
Comment: DOS Setup
run start Wed Sep 27 17:47:09 2000
run finish Wed Sep 27 17:54:19 2000
drive 0x80 (master) no BIOS extensions
```

```
3330432 sectors wiped with D1
```
2. partition(src,1,*,Fat 12)
3. partition(src,2,*,Small Fat 16)
4. load_os(DOS)

```
Comment: beta5 D1 (DOS) Layout
Source disk partition table
P 000000063 000024129 0000/001/01 0005/063/63 Boot 01 Fat12
X 000024192 003306240 0006/000/01 0825/063/63      05 extended
S 000000063 000044289 0006/001/01 0016/063/63      04 Fat16
x 000044352 003261888 0017/000/01 0825/063/63      05 extended
S 000000063 003261825 0017/001/01 0825/063/63      06 Fat16
Source disk layout:  00826/064/63 3330432 total sectors on disk
        Start LBA    End LBA    Length    Size: MB    (binary)
  0 B         0         62        63      0.03MB      0.03BMB
  1 P        63      24191     24129     12.35MB     11.78BMB
  2 b     24192      24254        63      0.03MB      0.03BMB
  3 P     24255      68543     44289     22.68MB     21.63BMB
  4 b     68544      68606        63      0.03MB      0.03BMB
  5 P     68607    3330431   3261825   1670.05MB   1592.69BMB
```

5. before=hash(src)

```
A:\DISKHASH.EXE @(#) Version 2.1 Created 09/27/00 at 13:44:51
Comment: hash D1 before running SafeBack
run start Fri Sep 29 11:06:09 2000
run finish Fri Sep 29 12:09:44 2000
drive 0x80 (master) no BIOS extensions
Disk SHA-1 hash 305B31403D8AD36BCB9AF108821818DCFA3F919A
```

6. wipe(img)
7. partition(img,1,MAX,Big Fat 16)
8. wipe(dst)

```
A:\DISKWIPE.EXE @(#) Version 2.2 Created 10/02/00 at 09:08:26
Comment: Beta4, Wipe D2 (setup for partition copy tests)
run start Mon Oct 23 11:26:16 2000
run finish Mon Oct 23 11:33:38 2000
drive 0x80 (master) no BIOS extensions
3330432 sectors wiped with D2
```

9. partition(dst,1,x,type(src.1)) size(src.1) > x
   Execute
10. image(src.1,img.1)

```
         SafeBack 2.0 31Jan00 execution started on Oct 24, 2000 14:29.
14:30:04  Menu selections:
             Function:             Backup
             Remote connection:    Local
             Direct access:        No
             Use XBIOS:            Auto
             Adjust partitions:    Auto
             Backfill on restore:  Yes
             Compress sector data: Yes
14:32:37  Backup file D:\DI-60.001 created.
          Backup file comment record:
             Beta2 DI-60 D1==>D2
14:33:04  Backing up drive C:
          to D:\DI-60.001 on Oct 24, 2000 14:33
14:33:06  Local SafeBack is running on DOS 6.30
          Source drive C:
             Capacity........12 MB
```

```
              Cylinders.......5
              Heads...........64
14:33:14   Backup file CRC: a5e680fd.
14:33:14   Backup of drive C: completed on Oct 24, 2000 14:33.
           SafeBack execution ended on Oct 24, 2000 14:33.
```

11. load(img.1,dst.1)

```
           SafeBack 2.0 31Jan00 execution started on Oct 24, 2000 14:34.
14:34:35   Menu selections:
              Function:              Restore
              Remote connection:     Local
              Direct access:         No
              Use XBIOS:             Auto
              Adjust partitions:     Auto
              Backfill on restore:   Yes
              Compress sector data:  Yes
14:34:54   Backup file created on Oct 24, 2000 14:33
           by Gary Fisher Natl Institute of Standards & Technology Software
Diagnostics & Con
           Backup file comment record:
              Beta2 DI-60 D1==>D2
14:34:55   Backup file D:\DI-60.001 opened for access.
14:36:07   The destination drive capacity is smaller than that of the
           original source drive.
14:36:20   Partition/Boot information saved to A:\PT-DI-60.SPS.
14:36:21   Restore of drive C: from D:\DI-60.001
           to drive G: started on Oct 24, 2000 14:36
14:36:21   Local SafeBack is running on DOS 6.30
           Source drive C:
              Capacity........12 MB
              Cylinders.......5
              Heads...........64
           Destination drive G:
              Capacity........10 MB
              Cylinders.......4
              Heads...........64
14:36:36   Restore of drive C: to drive G: completed on Oct 24, 2000 14:36
14:36:43   Menu selections:
              Function:              Restore
              Remote connection:     Local
              Direct access:         No
              Use XBIOS:             Auto
              Adjust partitions:     Auto
              Backfill on restore:   Yes
              Compress sector data:  Yes
           SafeBack execution ended on Oct 24, 2000 14:36.
```

Measure

12. after=hash(src)

```
A:\DISKHASH.EXE @(#) Version 2.2 Created 10/02/00 at 09:08:26
Comment: beta5 hash disk after DI-21
run start Mon Nov 20 11:41:49 2000
run finish Mon Nov 20 12:02:03 2000
drive 0x80 (master) no BIOS extensions
Disk SHA-1 hash 305B31403D8AD36BCB9AF108821818DCFA3F919A
```

13. Examine_message(Destination too small)

```
14:36:07   The destination drive capacity is smaller than that of the
           original source drive.
```

14. Compare(src.1,dst.1)

   Output Specifications (expected results)

15. before=after

```
before = 305B31403D8AD36BCB9AF108821818DCFA3F919A
after  = 305B31403D8AD36BCB9AF108821818DCFA3F919A
```

16. Destination too small message

```
14:36:07  The destination drive capacity is smaller than that of the
          original source drive.
```

17. src and dst compare equal

```
sectors compared 20097 match 20097 differ 0 dropped 4032
```

Test case ID DI-61

Test assertions

21.   If a duplicate destination partition is created from an image file of a larger source partition, then each sector of the destination partition must compare equal to the LBA corresponding sector of the source partition.

22.   If a duplicate destination partition is created from an image file of a larger source partition, then the tool must notify the user.

28.   The source before using the tool must be equal to the source after tool use.

29.   The results of any remote tool use must be equal to the results of local identical tool use.

   Setup

1. wipe(src)

```
A:\DISKWIPE.EXE @(#) Version 2.1 Created 09/27/00 at 13:44:51
Comment: Windows 95 setup
run start Wed Sep 27 17:52:35 2000
run finish Wed Sep 27 17:59:47 2000
drive 0x80 (master) no BIOS extensions
3330432 sectors wiped with F1
```

2. partition(src,1,*,Big Fat 16)

3. load_os(Windows 95)

```
Comment: beta5 F1 W95 layout
Source disk partition table
P 000000063 003072321 0000/001/01 0761/063/63 Boot 06 Fat16
X 003072384 000258048 0762/000/01 0825/063/63      05 extended
S 000000063 000104769 0762/001/01 0787/063/63      06 Fat16
x 000104832 000153216 0788/000/01 0825/063/63      05 extended
S 000000063 000153153 0788/001/01 0825/063/63      06 Fat16
Source disk layout:  00826/064/63 3330432 total sectors on disk
        Start LBA    End LBA    Length    Size: MB    (binary)
  0 B          0         62        63      0.03MB      0.03BMB
  1 P         63    3072383   3072321   1573.03MB   1500.16BMB
  2 b    3072384    3072446        63      0.03MB      0.03BMB
  3 P    3072447    3177215    104769     53.64MB     51.16BMB
  4 b    3177216    3177278        63      0.03MB      0.03BMB
  5 P    3177279    3330431    153153     78.41MB     74.78BMB
```

4. before=hash(src)

```
A:\DISKHASH.EXE @(#) Version 2.2 Created 10/02/00 at 09:08:26
Comment: rehash F1 (Win 95)
run start Fri Nov 03 14:08:19 2000
run finish Fri Nov 03 14:28:46 2000
drive 0x80 (master) no BIOS extensions
Disk SHA-1 hash 5FBEEB219E7282ED621645A67252A70F4D8BBF21
```

5. wipe(img)

6. partition(img,1,MAX,Big Fat 16)
7. wipe(dst)
```
A:\DISKWIPE.EXE @(#) Version 2.2 Created 10/02/00 at 09:08:26
Comment: Beta5 DI-33,40,54,61 (partition operations)
run start Tue Nov 28 11:57:54 2000
run finish Tue Nov 28 12:05:34 2000
drive 0x80 (master) no BIOS extensions
3330432 sectors wiped with D2
```
8. partition(dst,1,x,type(src.1)) size(src.1) > x
   Execute
9. establish_link()
10. image(src.1,img.1)
```
            SafeBack 2.0 31Jan00 execution started on Nov 28, 2000 13:54.
13:54:34    Menu selections:
                Function:              Backup
                Remote connection:     LPT1:
                Direct access:         No
                Use XBIOS:             Auto
                Adjust partitions:     Auto
                Backfill on restore:   Yes
                Compress sector data:  Yes
13:55:03    Backup file K:\F1T61.001 created.
            Backup file comment record:
                remote beta3 F1(D)->D3->D2 (beta2)
13:56:00    Backing up drive D:
            to K:\F1T61.001 on Nov 28, 2000 13:56
13:56:02    Local SafeBack is running on DOS 6.30
13:56:02    Remote SafeBack server is running on DOS 6.30
            Source drive D:
                Capacity........51 MB
                Cylinders.......25
                Heads...........64
14:11:07    Backup file CRC: 637f6c7c.
14:11:07    Backup of drive D: completed on Nov 28, 2000 14:11.
            SafeBack execution ended on Nov 28, 2000 14:11.
```
11. load(img.1,dst.1)
```
            SafeBack 2.0 31Jan00 execution started on Nov 28, 2000 14:29.
14:30:11    Menu selections:
                Function:              Restore
                Remote connection:     Local
                Direct access:         No
                Use XBIOS:             Auto
                Adjust partitions:     Auto
                Backfill on restore:   Yes
                Compress sector data:  Yes
14:30:28    Backup file created on Nov 28, 2000 13:56
            by Gary Fisher Natl Institute of Standards & Technology Software
Diagnostics & Con
            Backup file comment record:
                remote beta3 F1(D)->D3->D2 (beta2)
14:30:37    Backup file K:\F1T61.001 opened for access.
14:30:50    The destination drive capacity is smaller than that of the
            original source drive.
14:31:09    Partition/Boot information saved to A:\PT-DI-61.SPS.
14:31:09    Restore of drive D: from K:\F1T61.001
            to drive H: started on Nov 28, 2000 14:31
```

```
14:31:09   Local SafeBack is running on DOS 6.30
           Source drive D:
               Capacity........51 MB
               Cylinders.......25
               Heads..........64
           Destination drive H:
               Capacity........43 MB
               Cylinders.......21
               Heads..........64
14:31:34   Restore of drive D: to drive H: completed on Nov 28, 2000 14:31
14:31:45   Menu selections:
               Function:             Restore
               Remote connection:    Local
               Direct access:        No
               Use XBIOS:            Auto
               Adjust partitions:    Auto
               Backfill on restore:  Yes
               Compress sector data: Yes
           SafeBack execution ended on Nov 28, 2000 14:31.
```

Measure

12. after=hash(src)

```
A:\DISKHASH.EXE %Z% Version %I% Created %G% at %U%
Comment: beta5 hash F1 after DI-02,14,33,40,54,61
run start Tue Nov 28 15:03:27 2000
run finish Tue Nov 28 15:24:20 2000
drive 0x80 (master) no BIOS extensions
Disk SHA-1 hash 5FBEEB219E7282ED621645A67252A70F4D8BBF21
```

13. Examine_message(Destination too small)

```
14:30:50   The destination drive capacity is smaller than that of the
           original source drive.
```

14. Compare(src.1,dst.1)

Output Specifications (expected results)

15. before=after

```
before = 5FBEEB219E7282ED621645A67252A70F4D8BBF21
after  = 5FBEEB219E7282ED621645A67252A70F4D8BBF21
```

16. Destination too small message

```
14:30:50   The destination drive capacity is smaller than that of the
           original source drive.
```

17. src and dst compare equal

```
sectors compared 88641 match 88641 differ 0 dropped 16128
```

Test case ID DI-67

Test assertions

28.   The source before using the tool must be equal to the source after tool use.

32.   If the tool has a feature to verify the integrity of the image file, the tool shall detect and identify the anomaly and notify the user if the image file has been changed.

Setup

1. DI-15

Execute

2. verify(img.1)

```
        SafeBack 2.0 31Jan00 execution started on Nov 14, 2000 18:08.
```

```
18:09:02  Menu selections:
           Function:              Verify
           Remote connection:     Local
           Direct access:         No
           Use XBIOS:             Auto
           Adjust partitions:     Auto
           Backfill on restore:   Yes
           Compress sector data:  Yes
18:10:57  Backup file created on Nov 14, 2000 11:25
           by Gary Fisher Natl Institute of Standards & Technology Software
Diagnostics & Con
           Backup file comment record:
             Beta3 DI-15 F2->D3->D11  Fill, NO adjust
18:11:04  Backup file E:\F2T15.001 opened for access.
18:11:04  Verify of drive 0:
           from E:\F2T15.001 started on Nov 14, 2000 18:11.
18:11:04  Local SafeBack is running on DOS 6.30
           Source drive 0:
             Capacity........1628 MB
             Cylinders.......827
             Heads..........64
18:18:35  The whole-file CRC verifies:  82d57464
18:18:35  Verify of backup data for drive 0: completed on Nov 14, 2000 18:18.
18:18:55  Menu selections:
           Function:              Verify
           Remote connection:     Local
           Direct access:         No
           Use XBIOS:             Auto
           Adjust partitions:     Auto
           Backfill on restore:   Yes
           Compress sector data:  Yes
           SafeBack execution ended on Nov 14, 2000 18:19.
```

Measure
3. Examine_message(Image file verifies)
```
18:18:35  The whole-file CRC verifies:  82d57464
```
Output Specifications (expected results)
4. Image verifies message
```
18:18:35  The whole-file CRC verifies:  82d57464
```

Test case ID DI-69

Test assertions

27.   If the tool is able to create a destination from an image file that contains read errors, the destination sectors corresponding to the unreadable data must be treated as fill sectors (the tool may allow a specified action or may fill the sectors with zeros).

28.   The source before using the tool must be equal to the source after tool use.

32.   If the tool has a feature to verify the integrity of the image file, the tool shall detect and identify the anomaly and notify the user if the image file has been changed.

Setup
1. DI-15
   Execute
2. corrupt(img)
3. verify(img.1)
```
           SafeBack 2.0 31Jan00 execution started on Nov 14, 2000 19:01.
```

```
19:01:54  Menu selections:
              Function:            Verify
              Remote connection:   Local
              Direct access:       No
              Use XBIOS:           Auto
              Adjust partitions:   Auto
              Backfill on restore: Yes
              Compress sector data: Yes
19:02:17  Backup file created on Nov 14, 2000 11:25
              by Gary Fisher Natl Institute of Standards & Technology Software
Diagnostics & Con
              Backup file comment record:
                  Beta3 DI-15 F2->D3->D11  Fill, NO adjust
19:02:19  Backup file E:\F2T15.001 opened for access.
19:02:19  Verify of drive 0:
              from E:\F2T15.001 started on Nov 14, 2000 19:02.
19:02:19  Local SafeBack is running on DOS 6.30
              Source drive 0:
                  Capacity........1628 MB
                  Cylinders.......827
                  Heads...........64
19:03:31  F2T15.001, record 546686 has a CRC error. a038 was expected, but 36fa
read.
19:06:13  Backup file CRC error ignored by recovery at sector 546686.
19:12:33  CRC mismatch:  Calculated: 9be950f5, Read: 82d57464
19:16:03  Verify of backup data for drive 0: completed on Nov 14, 2000 19:16.
19:18:22  Menu selections:
              Function:            Verify
              Remote connection:   Local
              Direct access:       No
              Use XBIOS:           Auto
              Adjust partitions:   Auto
              Backfill on restore: Yes
              Compress sector data: Yes
              SafeBack execution ended on Nov 14, 2000 19:18.
```
Measure

4. Examine_message(Corrupt image file)
```
19:03:31  F2T15.001, record 546686 has a CRC error. a038 was expected, but 36fa
read.
```
Output Specifications (expected results)

5. Corrupt image file message
```
19:03:31  F2T15.001, record 546686 has a CRC error. a038 was expected, but 36fa
read.
```

Test case ID DI-70

Test assertions

28.   The source before using the tool must be equal to the source after tool use.

32.   If the tool has a feature to verify the integrity of the image file, the tool shall detect and identify the anomaly and notify the user if the image file has been changed.

Setup

1. DI-47

Execute

2. verify(img.1)
```
          SafeBack 2.0 31Jan00 execution started on Nov 17, 2000 10:22.
```

```
10:22:10  Menu selections:
            Function:            Verify
            Remote connection:   Local
            Direct access:       No
            Use XBIOS:           Auto
            Adjust partitions:   Auto
            Backfill on restore: Yes
            Compress sector data: Yes
10:22:24  Backup file created on Nov 17, 2000 09:44
            by Gary Fisher Natl Institute of Standards & Technology Software
Diagnostics & Con
            Backup file comment record:
              Beta2 DI-47 F1:E->D7:E\F1T47->D7
10:22:29  Backup file D:\F1T47.001 opened for access.
10:22:29  Verify of drive E:
            from D:\F1T47.001 started on Nov 17, 2000 10:22.
10:22:29  Local SafeBack is running on DOS 6.30
            Source drive E:
              Capacity........51 MB
              Cylinders.......25
              Heads...........64
10:22:46  The whole-file CRC verifies:  147646cf
10:22:46  Verify of backup data for drive E: completed on Nov 17, 2000 10:22.
10:22:56  Menu selections:
            Function:            Verify
            Remote connection:   Local
            Direct access:       No
            Use XBIOS:           Auto
            Adjust partitions:   Auto
            Backfill on restore: Yes
            Compress sector data: Yes
            SafeBack execution ended on Nov 17, 2000 10:23.
```
   Measure
3. Examine_message(Image file verifies)
```
10:22:46  The whole-file CRC verifies:  147646cf
```
   Output Specifications (expected results)
4. Image verifies message
```
10:22:46  The whole-file CRC verifies:  147646cf
```

Test case ID DI-71

Test assertions

27.   If the tool is able to create a destination from an image file that contains read errors, the destination sectors corresponding to the unreadable data must be treated as fill sectors (the tool may allow a specified action or may fill the sectors with zeros).

28.   The source before using the tool must be equal to the source after tool use.

32.   If the tool has a feature to verify the integrity of the image file, the tool shall detect and identify the anomaly and notify the user if the image file has been changed.

   Setup
1. DI-47
   Execute
2. corrupt(img)
3. verify(img.1)
```
          SafeBack 2.0 31Jan00 execution started on Nov 17, 2000 11:02.
```

```
11:02:55  Menu selections:
              Function:            Verify
              Remote connection:   Local
              Direct access:       No
              Use XBIOS:           Auto
              Adjust partitions:   Auto
              Backfill on restore: Yes
              Compress sector data: Yes
11:03:14  Backup file created on Nov 17, 2000 09:44
          by Gary Fisher Natl Institute of Standards & Technology Software
Diagnostics & Con
          Backup file comment record:
              Beta2 DI-47 F1:E->D7:E\F1T47->D7
11:03:18  Backup file D:\F1T47.001 opened for access.
11:03:18  Verify of drive E:
          from D:\F1T47.001 started on Nov 17, 2000 11:03.
11:03:18  Local SafeBack is running on DOS 6.30
          Source drive E:
              Capacity........51 MB
              Cylinders.......25
              Heads...........64
11:03:18  F1T47.001, record 238 has a CRC error. 8bc2 was expected, but 7444
read.
11:03:26  Backup file CRC error ignored by recovery at sector 238.
11:03:43  CRC mismatch:  Calculated: d5066291, Read: 147646cf
11:03:46  Verify of backup data for drive E: completed on Nov 17, 2000 11:03.
11:04:05  Menu selections:
              Function:            Verify
              Remote connection:   Local
              Direct access:       No
              Use XBIOS:           Auto
              Adjust partitions:   Auto
              Backfill on restore: Yes
              Compress sector data: Yes
          SafeBack execution ended on Nov 17, 2000 11:04.
```

Measure

4. Examine_message(Corrupt image file)

```
11:03:18  F1T47.001, record 238 has a CRC error. 8bc2 was expected, but 7444
read.
```

Output Specifications (expected results)

5. Corrupt image file message

```
11:03:18  F1T47.001, record 238 has a CRC error. 8bc2 was expected, but 7444
read.
```

Test case ID DI-73

Test assertions

28. *The source before using the tool must be equal to the source after tool use.*

29. *The results of any remote tool use must be equal to the results of local identical tool use.*

30. *If deleted files exist that are recoverable on the source, then these files must be recoverable on the destination.*

Setup

1. DI-21

Execute

2. recover_files()

```
Test DI-73

Start with D2 after Test DI-21
D2 is bit for bit identical to D1
D1 has a subdirectory, UDT with the following deleted files:
     (1) udt\gone.txt
     (2) udt\sub (a directory)
     (3) udt\sub\missing.txt

Boot d2
cd c:\udt
dir >before.txt
undelete gone.txt, sub and sub\missing.txt
dir >after.txt

Original.txt is the output of the dir command
on the original files used to create the udt
directory.

udt-set.bat is the batch file used to create
the udt directory (using the files described
```

in original.txt. Measure
3. Examine_results()

```
Directory before recovery:

 Volume in drive C is PCDOS_6
 Volume Serial Number is 293C-5320

 Directory of C:\UDT
.              <DIR>         09-28-00    1:47p
..             <DIR>         09-28-00    1:47p
README   TXT           319 09-28-00   12:54p
!ACK     TXT         8,846 09-28-00   12:58p
        4 file(s)          9,165 bytes

                    8,908,800 bytes free

Directory after recovery:

 Volume in drive C is PCDOS_6
 Volume Serial Number is 293C-5320


Directory of C:\UDT

.              <DIR>         09-28-00    1:47p
..             <DIR>         09-28-00    1:47p
README   TXT           319 09-28-00   12:54p
!ACK     TXT         8,846 09-28-00   12:58p
SUB            <DIR>         09-28-00    1:47p
GONE     TXT         2,975 09-28-00   12:56p
        6 file(s)         12,140 bytes
```

```
Directory of C:\UDT\SUB

.                <DIR>         09-28-00   1:47p
..               <DIR>         09-28-00   1:47p
MISSING  TXT      11,153 09-28-00   1:00p
        3 file(s)        11,153 bytes


Total files listed:
        9 file(s)        23,293 bytes
                      8,892,416 bytes free
```

Output Specifications (expected results)
4. Files recovered

```
Directory before recovery:

 Volume in drive C is PCDOS_6
 Volume Serial Number is 293C-5320

 Directory of C:\UDT

.                <DIR>         09-28-00   1:47p
..               <DIR>         09-28-00   1:47p
README   TXT         319 09-28-00  12:54p
!ACK     TXT       8,846 09-28-00  12:58p
        4 file(s)         9,165 bytes
                      8,908,800 bytes free

Directory after recovery:

 Volume in drive C is PCDOS_6
 Volume Serial Number is 293C-5320

Directory of C:\UDT

.                <DIR>         09-28-00   1:47p
..               <DIR>         09-28-00   1:47p
README   TXT         319 09-28-00  12:54p
!ACK     TXT       8,846 09-28-00  12:58p
SUB              <DIR>         09-28-00   1:47p
GONE     TXT       2,975 09-28-00  12:56p
        6 file(s)        12,140 bytes


Directory of C:\UDT\SUB

.                <DIR>         09-28-00   1:47p
..               <DIR>         09-28-00   1:47p
MISSING  TXT      11,153 09-28-00   1:00p
        3 file(s)        11,153 bytes


Total files listed:
        9 file(s)        23,293 bytes
                      8,892,416 bytes free
```

Test case ID DI-74

Test assertions

28.   The source before using the tool must be equal to the source after tool use.

31.   If the logical disk as presented by the BIOS is smaller than the physical disk, then the tool must not access any sectors outside the logical disk.

Setup

1. wipe(src)

```
A:\DISKWIPE.EXE @(#) Version 2.1 Created 09/27/00 at 13:44:51
Comment: initial setup for NT
run start Wed Sep 27 14:37:32 2000
run finish Wed Sep 27 14:44:44 2000
drive 0x80 (master) no BIOS extensions
3330432 sectors wiped with D9
```

2. partition(src,1,*,NTFS)

3. load_os(Windows NT)

```
Comment: beta5 D9 (NT) layout
Source disk partition table
P 000000063 003072321 0000/001/01 0761/063/63 Boot 07 NTFS
X 003072384 000262080 0762/000/01 0826/063/63      05 extended
S 000000063 000060417 0762/001/01 0776/063/63      07 NTFS
x 000060480 000080640 0777/000/01 0796/063/63      05 extended
S 000000063 000080577 0777/001/01 0796/063/63      07 NTFS
x 000141120 000120960 0797/000/01 0826/063/63      05 extended
S 000000063 000120897 0797/001/01 0826/063/63      07 NTFS
Source disk layout:   00826/064/63 3330432 total sectors on disk
     Start LBA    End LBA    Length   Size: MB   (binary)
 0 B         0         62        63    0.03MB    0.03BMB
 1 P        63    3072383   3072321 1573.03MB 1500.16BMB
 2 b   3072384    3072446        63    0.03MB    0.03BMB
 3 P   3072447    3132863     60417   30.93MB   29.50BMB
 4 b   3132864    3132926        63    0.03MB    0.03BMB
 5 P   3132927    3213503     80577   41.26MB   39.34BMB
 6 b   3213504    3213566        63    0.03MB    0.03BMB
 7 P   3213567    3334463    120897   61.90MB   59.03BMB
```

4. before=hash(src)

```
A:\DISKHASH.EXE @(#) Version 2.1 Created 09/27/00 at 13:44:51
Comment: Reference hash on D9 (NTFS)
run start Fri Sep 29 11:21:28 2000
run finish Fri Sep 29 12:26:11 2000
drive 0x80 (master) no BIOS extensions
Disk SHA-1 hash A683672031589F08895F3AEDE8DBC77718648284
```

5. wipe(dst)

6. wipe_extra(src)

```
A:\DISKWIPE.EXE @(#) Version 2.2 Created 10/02/00 at 09:08:26
Comment: beta5 Setup extra tracks on D9
run start Mon Nov 20 16:00:53 2000
run finish Mon Nov 20 16:01:51 2000
drive 0x80 (master) no BIOS extensions
```

7. wipe_extra(dst)

Execute

8. copy(src,dst,f,n)

Measure

9. after=hash(src)

10. Compare(src,dst)
Comment: beta3 DI-74 using D9/D11 from DI-04
run start Tue Nov 21 11:22:04 2000
run finish Tue Nov 21 11:51:43 2000
sectors compared 3335472 match 3334464 differ 1008 dropped 0
filled: zero 9307683 src 0 dst 0 other 0 remainder 0

11. examine_extra(dst)
   Output Specifications (expected results)

12. before=after
before = A683672031589F08895F3AEDE8DBC77718648284
after =

13. src and dst compare equal
sectors compared 3335472 match 3334464 differ 1008 dropped 0

14. excess dst sectors zero filled
filled: zero 9307683 src 0 dst 0 other 0 remainder 0

15. No extra source sectors on dst

Test case ID DI-75

Test assertions

28.   The source before using the tool must be equal to the source after tool use.

33.   If a duplicate copy is created directly, without using the BIOS, from a source disk of the same geometry, then the disks must compare equal.

   Setup

1. wipe(src)
A:\DISKWIPE.EXE @(#) Version 2.1 Created 09/27/00 at 13:44:51
Comment: DOS Setup
run start Wed Sep 27 17:47:09 2000
run finish Wed Sep 27 17:54:19 2000
drive 0x80 (master) no BIOS extensions
3330432 sectors wiped with D1

2. partition(src,1,*,Fat 12)

3. partition(src,2,*,Small Fat 16)

4. load_os(DOS)
Comment: beta5 D1 (DOS) Layout
Source disk partition table
P 000000063 000024129 0000/001/01 0005/063/63 Boot 01 Fat12
X 000024192 003306240 0006/000/01 0825/063/63   05 extended
S 000000063 000044289 0006/001/01 0016/063/63   04 Fat16
x 000044352 003261888 0017/000/01 0825/063/63   05 extended
S 000000063 003261825 0017/001/01 0825/063/63   06 Fat16
Source disk layout: 00826/064/63 3330432 total sectors on disk
      Start LBA   End LBA   Length   Size: MB   (binary)
  0 B   0   62   63   0.03MB   0.03BMB
  1 P   63   24191   24129   12.35MB   11.78BMB
  2 b   24192   24254   63   0.03MB   0.03BMB
  3 P   24255   68543   44289   22.68MB   21.63BMB
  4 b   68544   68606   63   0.03MB   0.03BMB
  5 P   68607   3330431   3261825 1670.05MB 1592.69BMB

5. before=hash(src)
A:\DISKHASH.EXE @(#) Version 2.1 Created 09/27/00 at 13:44:51
Comment: hash D1 before running SafeBack
run start Fri Sep 29 11:06:09 2000

```
run finish Fri Sep 29 12:09:44 2000
drive 0x80 (master) no BIOS extensions
Disk SHA-1 hash 305B31403D8AD36BCB9AF108821818DCFA3F919A
```
6. wipe(dst)
```
A:\DISKWIPE.EXE @(#) Version 2.2 Created 10/02/00 at 09:08:26
Comment: beta5 DI-75 setup
run start Fri Nov 17 14:25:58 2000
run finish Fri Nov 17 14:33:26 2000
drive 0x80 (master) no BIOS extensions
3330432 sectors wiped with D2
```
Execute

7. copy(src,dst,direct)
```
         SafeBack 2.0 31Jan00 execution started on Nov 17, 2000 15:42.
15:43:21  Menu selections:
             Function:              Copy
             Remote connection:     Local
             Direct access:         Yes
             Use XBIOS:             Auto
             Adjust partitions:     Auto
             Backfill on restore:   Yes
             Compress sector data:  Yes
15:43:36  Copy from Local drive 0: to local drive 1:
15:43:46  Copy of Local drive 0: to drive 1: begun on Nov 17, 2000 15:43
15:43:46  Local SafeBack is running on DOS 6.30
15:43:46  Partition table for drive 0:
          Source drive 0:
            Capacity........1629 MB
            Cylinders.......3309
            Heads...........16
            Model: QUANTUM SIROCCO1700A
            Serial Number: 111615915557
            Firmware version: A01.0000
            IDE controller port with LBA direct drive access used.
          Destination drive 1:
            Capacity........1629 MB
            Cylinders.......3309
            Heads...........16
            Model: QUANTUM SIROCCO1700A
            Serial Number: 111614919955
            Firmware version: A01.0000
            IDE controller port with LBA direct drive access used.
15:55:34  Partition table for drive 1:
15:55:35  Copy of drive 0: to drive 1: completed on Nov 17, 2000 15:55
          SafeBack execution ended on Nov 17, 2000 15:56.
```
Measure

8. after=hash(src)
```
A:\DISKHASH.EXE @(#) Version 2.2 Created 10/02/00 at 09:08:26
Comment: Beta5 hash after DI-76
run start Fri Nov 17 18:21:47 2000
run finish Fri Nov 17 18:42:23 2000
drive 0x80 (master) no BIOS extensions
Disk SHA-1 hash 305B31403D8AD36BCB9AF108821818DCFA3F919A
```
9. Compare(src,dst)
```
Comment: DI-75 Beta3
run start Fri Nov 17 16:01:11 2000
run finish Fri Nov 17 16:12:28 2000
sectors compared 3335472 match 3335472 differ 0 dropped 0
```

```
filled: zero 0 src 0 dst 0 other 0 remainder 0
```
Output Specifications (expected results)

10. before=after
```
before = 305B31403D8AD36BCB9AF108821818DCFA3F919A
after  = 305B31403D8AD36BCB9AF108821818DCFA3F919A
```
11. src and dst compare equal
```
sectors compared 3335472 match 3335472 differ 0 dropped 0
```

Test case ID DI-76

Test assertions

28. *The source before using the tool must be equal to the source after tool use.*

35. *If a duplicate copy is created directly, without using the BIOS, from a source disk with the destination disk having a smaller geometry, then the tool must notify the user.*

Setup

1. wipe(src)
```
A:\DISKWIPE.EXE @(#) Version 2.1 Created 09/27/00 at 13:44:51
Comment: Windows 95 setup
run start Wed Sep 27 17:52:35 2000
run finish Wed Sep 27 17:59:47 2000
drive 0x80 (master) no BIOS extensions
3330432 sectors wiped with F1
```
2. partition(src,1,*,Big Fat 16)

3. load_os(Windows 95)
```
Comment: beta5 F1 W95 layout
Source disk partition table
P 000000063 003072321 0000/001/01 0761/063/63 Boot 06 Fat16
X 003072384 000258048 0762/000/01 0825/063/63      05 extended
S 000000063 000104769 0762/001/01 0787/063/63      06 Fat16
x 000104832 000153216 0788/000/01 0825/063/63      05 extended
S 000000063 000153153 0788/001/01 0825/063/63      06 Fat16
Source disk layout:  00826/064/63 3330432 total sectors on disk
      Start LBA    End LBA    Length    Size: MB    (binary)
  0 B         0         62        63     0.03MB     0.03BMB
  1 P        63    3072383   3072321  1573.03MB  1500.16BMB
  2 b   3072384    3072446        63     0.03MB     0.03BMB
  3 P   3072447    3177215    104769    53.64MB    51.16BMB
  4 b   3177216    3177278        63     0.03MB     0.03BMB
  5 P   3177279    3330431    153153    78.41MB    74.78BMB
```
4. before=hash(src)
```
A:\DISKHASH.EXE @(#) Version 2.2 Created 10/02/00 at 09:08:26
Comment: rehash F1 (Win 95)
run start Fri Nov 03 14:08:19 2000
run finish Fri Nov 03 14:28:46 2000
drive 0x80 (master) no BIOS extensions
Disk SHA-1 hash 5FBEEB219E7282ED621645A67252A70F4D8BBF21
```
5. wipe(dst)
```
A:\DISKWIPE.EXE @(#) Version 2.2 Created 10/02/00 at 09:08:26
Comment: beta5 DI-76
run start Fri Nov 17 16:05:02 2000
run finish Fri Nov 17 16:19:51 2000
drive 0x80 (master) no BIOS extensions
2495808 sectors wiped with D5
```
Execute

6. copy(src,dst,direct)

```
          SafeBack 2.0 31Jan00 execution started on Nov 17, 2000 16:39.
16:39:35  Menu selections:
              Function:              Copy
              Remote connection:     Local
              Direct access:         Yes
              Use XBIOS:             Auto
              Adjust partitions:     No
              Backfill on restore:   Yes
              Compress sector data:  Yes
16:40:03  Copy from Local drive 1: to local drive 0:
16:40:03  Insufficient destination file space projected.
16:40:23  Copy of Local drive 1: to drive 0: begun on Nov 17, 2000 16:40
16:40:23  Local SafeBack is running on DOS 6.30
16:40:23  Partition table for drive 1:
          Source drive 1:
              Capacity........1629 MB
              Cylinders.......3309
              Heads...........16
              Model: QUANTUM SIROCCO1700A
              Serial Number: 111615915557
              Firmware version: A01.0000
              IDE controller port with LBA direct drive access used.
          Destination drive 0:
              Capacity........1222 MB
              Cylinders.......2482
              Heads...........16
              Model: Seagate Technology 1275MB - ST31276A
              Serial Number:          FNH3HQL
              Firmware version: 1.35
              IDE controller port with LBA direct drive access used.
17:01:08  Copy of drive 1: to drive 0: completed on Nov 17, 2000 17:01
          SafeBack execution ended on Nov 17, 2000 17:10.
```

Measure

7. after=hash(src)

```
A:\DISKHASH.EXE @(#) Version 2.2 Created 10/02/00 at 09:08:26
Comment: beta5 DI-10 hash F1 after running SafeBack
run start Sun Nov 19 11:50:17 2000
run finish Sun Nov 19 12:10:50 2000
drive 0x80 (master) no BIOS extensions
Disk SHA-1 hash 5FBEEB219E7282ED621645A67252A70F4D8BBF21
```

8. Examine_message(Destination too small)

```
16:40:03  Insufficient destination file space projected.
```

9. Compare(src,dst)

```
Comment: beta2 DI-76
run start Fri Nov 17 17:11:21 2000
run finish Fri Nov 17 17:21:49 2000
sectors compared 2495808 match 2495808 differ 0 dropped 834624
filled: zero 0 src 0 dst 0 other 0 remainder 0
```

Output Specifications (expected results)

10. before=after

```
before = 5FBEEB219E7282ED621645A67252A70F4D8BBF21
after  = 5FBEEB219E7282ED621645A67252A70F4D8BBF21
```

11. Destination too small message

```
16:40:03  Insufficient destination file space projected.
```

12. src and dst compare equal
```
sectors compared 2495808 match 2495808 differ 0 dropped 834624
```

Test case DI-78

Test assertions
*1.   If a duplicate copy is created directly from a source disk of the same geometry, then the
disks must compare equal.*
28.   The source before using the tool must be equal to the source after tool use.
 Setup
    1. wipe(src)
```
A:\DISKWIPE.EXE @(#) Version 2.2 Created 10/02/00 at 09:08:26
Comment: DI-78 & DI-79 SCSI source setup
run start Tue Jan 30 16:01:28 2001
run finish Tue Jan 30 16:14:18 2001
drive 0x80 (master) use BIOS extensions
17921835 sectors wiped with C0
```
    2.   before=hash(src)
```
A:\DISKHASH.EXE @(#) Version 2.2 Created 10/02/00 at 09:08:26
Comment: DI-78, DI-79 hash SCSI before tests
run start Thu Feb 01 06:35:14 2001
run finish Thu Feb 01 11:37:14 2001
drive 0x80 (master) use BIOS extensions
Disk SHA-1 hash 26D2C0E8B9353F54DFEA007CFB3C476E30CABBD0
```
    3.   wipe(dst)
```
A:\DISKWIPE.EXE @(#) Version 2.2 Created 10/02/00 at 09:08:26
Comment: DI-78 wipe dst SCSI
run start Thu Feb 01 05:48:49 2001
run finish Thu Feb 01 06:02:06 2001
drive 0x81 (slave) use BIOS extensions
17921835 sectors wiped with 1C
```
    4. copy(src,dst)
```
            SafeBack 2.0 31Jan00 execution started on Feb  1, 2001 11:43.
11:43:48  Menu selections:
            Function:          Copy
            Remote connection: Local
            Direct access:     No
            Use XBIOS:         Yes
            Adjust partitions: No
            Backfill on restore: No
            Compress sector data: No

11:43:58  Copy from Local drive 0: to local drive 1:
11:44:10  Copy of Local drive 0: to drive 1: begun on Feb  1, 2001 11:44
11:44:10  Local SafeBack is running on DOS 6.30
            Source drive 0:
            Capacity........8751 MB
            Cylinders.......1115
            Heads..........255
            Sectors/Head....63
            Sector size.....512
            Destination drive 1:
            Capacity........8751 MB
            Cylinders.......1115
            Heads..........255
            Sectors/Head....63
```

```
            Sector size.....512
11:58:13  Copy of drive 0: to drive 1: completed on Feb  1, 2001 11:58

            SafeBack execution ended on Feb  1, 2001 12:21.
```
Measure
   5. after=hash(src)
```
A:\DISKHASH.EXE @(#) Version 2.2 Created 10/02/00 at 09:08:26
Comment: SCSI test DI-78, hash after SafeBack run.
run start Thu Feb 01 14:51:20 2001
run finish Thu Feb 01 19:55:27 2001
drive 0x80 (master) use BIOS extensions
Disk SHA-1 hash 26D2C0E8B9353F54DFEA007CFB3C476E30CABBD0
```
   6. Compare(src,dst)
```
A:\DISKCMP.EXE
version @(#) Version 2.3 Created 11/13/00 at 15:52:31
Comment: DI-78 scsi copy via bios
Sectors compared:      17921835
Sectors match:         17921835
Sectors differ:               0
run finish Thu Feb 01 13:03:21 2001
src drive 0x80 (master) use BIOS extensions
dst drive 0x81 (slave) use BIOS extensions
```
Output Specification
   7. before=after
```
before = 26D2C0E8B9353F54DFEA007CFB3C476E30CABBD0
after  = 26D2C0E8B9353F54DFEA007CFB3C476E30CABBD0
```
   8. src and dst compare equal
```
sectors compared 17921835 match 17921835 differ 0 dropped 0
```

Test case ID DI-79

28. The source before using the tool must be equal to the source after tool use.
33. If a duplicate copy is created directly, without using the BIOS, from a source disk of the same geometry, then the disks must compare equal.

   Setup
   1. wipe(src)
```
A:\DISKWIPE.EXE @(#) Version 2.2 Created 10/02/00 at 09:08:26
Comment: DI-78 & DI-79 SCSI source setup
run start Tue Jan 30 16:01:28 2001
run finish Tue Jan 30 16:14:18 2001
drive 0x80 (master) use BIOS extensions
17921835 sectors wiped with C0
```
   2. before=hash(src)
```
A:\DISKHASH.EXE @(#) Version 2.2 Created 10/02/00 at 09:08:26
Comment: DI-78, DI-79 hash SCSI before tests
run start Thu Feb 01 06:35:14 2001
run finish Thu Feb 01 11:37:14 2001
drive 0x80 (master) use BIOS extensions
Disk SHA-1 hash 26D2C0E8B9353F54DFEA007CFB3C476E30CABBD0
```
   3. wipe(dst)
```
A:\DISKWIPE.EXE @(#) Version 2.2 Created 10/02/00 at 09:08:26
Comment: DI-78 wipe dst SCSI
run start Thu Feb 01 05:48:49 2001
run finish Thu Feb 01 06:02:06 2001
drive 0x81 (slave) use BIOS extensions
```

```
17921835 sectors wiped with 1C
```
    Execute
1.   copy(src,dst,direct)

        SafeBack 2.0 31Jan00 execution started on Feb 2, 2001 07:40.

07:40:47 Menu selections:
            Function: Copy
            Remote connection: Local
            Direct access: Yes
            Use XBIOS: Auto
            Adjust partitions: Auto
            Backfill on restore: Yes
            Compress sector data: Yes

07:41:05 Copy from Local drive 0: to local drive 1:
07:41:15 Copy of Local drive 0: to drive 1: begun on Feb 2, 2001 07:41
07:41:15 Local SafeBack is running on DOS 6.30
            Source drive 0:
              Capacity........8751 MB
              Cylinders.......14384
              Heads...........3
              Sectors/Head....415
              Sector size.....512
              Model: SEAGATE ST39204LW
              Serial Number: 3BV0N0VW
              Firmware version: 0006
              SCSI ASPI driver direct drive access used.
            Destination drive 1:
              Capacity........8751 MB
              Cylinders.......14384
              Heads...........3
              Sectors/Head....415
              Sector size.....512
              Model: SEAGATE ST39204LW
              Serial Number: 3BV0NJ7F
              Firmware version: 0006
              SCSI ASPI driver direct drive access used.
07:52:43 Copy of drive 0: to drive 1: completed on Feb 2, 2001 07:52

        SafeBack execution ended on Feb 2, 2001 07:52.
    Measure
2.   after=hash(src)
A:\DISKHASH.EXE @(#) Version 2.2 Created 10/02/00 at 09:08:26
Comment: DI-79 hash after direct copy
run start Fri Feb 02 13:08:06 2001
run finish Fri Feb 02 18:09:55 2001
drive 0x80 (master) use BIOS extensions
Disk SHA-1 hash 26D2C0E8B9353F54DFEA007CFB3C476E30CABBD0
Normal exit A:\DISKHASH.EXE 16434495 sectors hashed
3.   Compare(src,dst)
A:\DISKCMP.EXE
version @(#) Version 2.3 Created 11/13/00 at 15:52:31
Comment: DI-79 SCSI direct copy
Sectors compared: 17921835
Sectors match: 2097270
Sectors differ: 15824565

```
run finish Fri Feb 02 08:49:06 2001
```
Output Specifications (expected results)

4.   before=after
```
before = 26D2C0E8B9353F54DFEA007CFB3C476E30CABBD0
after  = 26D2C0E8B9353F54DFEA007CFB3C476E30CABBD0
```
5.   src and dst compare equal
```
sectors compared 17921835 match 2097270 differ 15824565 dropped 0
```

About the National Institute of Justice

NIJ is the research, development, and evaluation agency of the U.S. Department of Justice. The Institute provides objective, independent, nonpartisan, evidence-based knowledge and tools to enhance the administration of justice and public safety. NIJ's principal authorities are derived from the Omnibus Crime Control and Safe Streets Act of 1968, as amended (see 42 U.S.C. §§ 3721–3723).

The NIJ Director is appointed by the President and confirmed by the Senate. The Director establishes the Institute's objectives, guided by the priorities of the Office of Justice Programs, the U.S. Department of Justice, and the needs of the field. The Institute actively solicits the views of criminal justice and other professionals and researchers to inform its search for the knowledge and tools to guide policy and practice.

Strategic Goals

NIJ has seven strategic goals grouped into three categories:

Creating relevant knowledge and tools

1. Partner with State and local practitioners and policymakers to identify social science research and technology needs.
2. Create scientific, relevant, and reliable knowledge—with a particular emphasis on terrorism, violent crime, drugs and crime, cost-effectiveness, and community-based efforts—to enhance the administration of justice and public safety.
3. Develop affordable and effective tools and technologies to enhance the administration of justice and public safety.

Dissemination

4. Disseminate relevant knowledge and information to practitioners and policymakers in an understandable, timely, and concise manner.
5. Act as an honest broker to identify the information, tools, and technologies that respond to the needs of stakeholders.

Agency management

6. Practice fairness and openness in the research and development process.
7. Ensure professionalism, excellence, accountability, cost-effectiveness, and integrity in the management and conduct of NIJ activities and programs.

Program Areas

In addressing these strategic challenges, the Institute is involved in the following program areas: crime control and prevention, including policing; drugs and crime; justice systems and offender behavior, including corrections; violence and victimization; communications and information technologies; critical incident response; investigative and forensic sciences, including DNA; less-than-lethal technologies; officer protection; education and training technologies; testing and standards; technology assistance to law enforcement and corrections agencies; field testing of promising programs; and international crime control.

In addition to sponsoring research and development and technology assistance, NIJ evaluates programs, policies, and technologies. NIJ communicates its research and evaluation findings through conferences and print and electronic media.

To find out more about the National Institute of Justice, please contact:

National Criminal Justice
 Reference Service
P.O. Box 6000
Rockville, MD 20849–6000
800–851–3420
e-mail: askncjrs@ncjrs.org